at home

Honey & Co.

Sarit Packer & Itamar Srulovich

at home

Middle Eastern recipes from our kitchen

Photography by Patricia Niven

PAVILION

To our siblings, Itay, Tammy
and Shai, with all our love

First published in the United Kingdom in 2018
by Pavilion
43 Great Ormond Street
London WC1N 3HZ

ISBN: 978-1-91159-566-3

A CIP catalogue record for this book is available from
the British Library.

10 9 8 7 6 5 4 3 2

Reproduction by Mission, Hong Kong
Printed and bound by 1010 Printing International Ltd,
  China

This book can be ordered direct from the publisher at
www.pavilionbooks.com

12 For us two

Potato and feta fritters

Harira soup

Green shakshuka

Saffron carrot soup with a little bit of rice

Mushroom scrambled eggs

Borlotti beans on toast with soft-boiled eggs

Steak fatoush salad with grapes and tomatoes

Chicken in plums and sweet spice

Israeli couscous with tomatoes, feta and lemon

Hedgehog meatballs

Lamb stew with medjool dates (and sometimes tahini)

Tinned tuna cakes

Arayes

Tagines

Lamb tagine with runner beans and tomatoes

Essaouira fish tagine

Prawn, pea and potato tagine

Coconut and lime pancakes with mango

Milk chocolate chip cookies with coffee beans

White chocolate chip, currant and orange cookies

Sumac and vanilla shortbread

58 For friends

Burning aubergines

Zaalouk

Silky green aubergine purée

Romanian white aubergine dip

Tuna dip with broccoli, potato and eggs

Baked artichokes with lemony ricotta dip

Baked goat's cheese wrapped in walnut pastry with fig relish

Pear and saffron salad with walnut tahini

Good sides

Roasted carrots with pistachio cream, coriander seeds and honey

Fennel, kohlrabi, orange and chilli salad

Fried cauliflower, amba and tahini

Brown wheat and broccoli salad with sesame dressing

Lentil stew with burnt aubergine, eggs, tahini and zehug

Spinach, egg and filo pie

Spring lamb meatballs with broad beans and courgettes

Yemeni lentil meatballs

Stuffed aubergine boats

Chicken braised in spicy matbucha and cracked wheat pilaf

Roasted duck legs with clementines and apricots

Quails with cannellini bean hummus, pepper and chilli butter

Feather blade braised with pumpkin, spices and prunes

Lemon and saffron posset

Chocolate cloud cake with red and black currants

Strawberry ricotta cakes

Chocolate financiers with coffee cream

122 For the weekend

Fig and feta pide

Turkish yogurt bread with aubergine filling

Jerusalem sesame bread

Harissa and lemon chicken sandwich

Roasted tomato and manouri cheese sandwich

Tuna, capers and roasted pepper sandwich

M'sabaha

Shishbarak

Celeriac mafrum

Honey and spice cookies

Medjool date, honey and macadamia breakfast loaf

Rich fruit cakes

Marmalade and dried fruit cake

Pistachio and cranberry cake

Pear and walnut upside-down cake

Summer weekends

Rabbit stifado

Pickled peach salad with pistachios and parsley

Cold tomato and basil soup with crispy pitta shards

Cold yogurt and pomegranate soup

Sardines with roasted tomatoes and crispy pitta

Frozen tahini parfait and chocolate sandwich cake

Frozen meringue bar with strawberry and lime

Baked custard fruit tart

188 For a crowd

Smoked haddock doughnuts

Taramosalata

Kamunia (a different kind of chopped liver)

Pumpkin chirshi

Fennel crackers with arak and sugar

Harissa and goat's cheese buns

Kalamata olive and orange maamool

Spiced butternut squash phylas

Roasted Romano peppers, chickpeas, olives, roasted tomatoes and cumin

Cherry, herb and freekeh tabule

Roasted spiced pumpkin with pickled apples

Red pepper, vine leaf and goat's cheese dolma cake

BBQ aubergine with jewelled rice salad

Fish pastilla

Chicken maklooba

Lamb chops with rocket, figs and walnuts

Royal mansaf

Tahini cake with lemon and white chocolate

Cherry pistachio Bakewell

Chocolate pecan slice with oranges

Marunchinos

Peanut and cocoa nib brittle

Pistachio, cardamom and rose marzipan

Donkey

256 For the kitchen

Sweet spice mix | Baharat spice mix | Ras el hanout spice mix | Amba spice mix | Amba relish | Amba sauce | Courgette pickle | Quince pickle | Kohlrabi pickle | Red pepper pickle | Red cabbage pickle | Green tahini | Chermoula paste | Shata | Pilpelchuma | Zehug coriander relish | Sweet zehug

276   Basic instructions (the way we work)

277   A few notes on ingredients

282   Index

288   Thank you

Salads and vegetable sides

73–4 Baked artichokes with lemony ricotta dip

78–9 Pear and saffron salad with walnut tahini

82 Roasted carrots with pistachio cream, coriander seeds and honey

84 Fennel, kohlrabi, orange and chilli salad

86 Fried cauliflower, amba and tahini

89 Brown wheat and broccoli salad with sesame dressing

169–70 Pickled peach salad with pistachios and parsley

210 Roasted Romano peppers, chickpeas, olives, roasted tomatoes and cumin

212 Cherry, herb and freekeh tabule

221–22 Jewelled rice salad

Snacks and dips

19 Potato and feta fritters

67 Zaalouk

69 Romanian white aubergine dip

69 Silky green aubergine purée

70 Tuna dip with broccoli, potato and eggs

73–4 Lemony ricotta dip

86 Tahini sauce

108–9 Cannellini bean hummus

142 Harissa and lemon chicken sandwich

143 Roasted tomato and manouri cheese sandwich

143 Tuna, capers and roasted pepper sandwich

172 Crispy pitta shards

195–96 Smoked haddock doughnuts

198 Taramosalata

200 Kamunia (a different kind of chopped liver)

201 Pumpkin chirshi

267 Courgette pickle

268 Kohlrabi pickle

268 Quince pickle

270 Red cabbage pickle

270 Red pepper pickle

272 Green tahini

Savoury bakes

76 Baked goat's cheese wrapped in walnut pastry with fig relish

128–29 Fig and feta pide

133–34 Turkish yogurt bread with aubergine filling

137–39 Jerusalem sesame bread

202 Fennel crackers with arak and sugar

204 Harissa and goat's cheese buns

206 Kalamata olive and orange maamool

209 Spiced butternut squash phylas

Vegetarian meals

26 Saffron carrot soup with a little bit of rice

36–7 Israeli couscous with tomatoes, feta and lemon

90–1 Lentil stew with burnt aubergine, eggs, tahini and zehug

93 Spinach, egg and filo pie

145–46 M'sabaha

172 Cold tomato and basil soup with crispy pitta shards

174–75 Cold yogurt and pomegranate soup

214–15 Roasted spiced pumpkin with pickled apples

217–18 Red pepper, vine leaf and goat's cheese dolma cake

221–22 BBQ aubergine with jewelled rice salad

Main meals

20–1 Harira soup

31 Steak fatoush salad with grapes and tomatoes

33–4 Chicken in plums and sweet spice

38 Hedgehog meatballs

40 Lamb stew with medjool dates (and sometimes tahini)

42 Tinned tuna cakes

45 Arayes

48 Lamb tagine with runner beans and tomatoes

49 Essaouira fish tagine

50 Prawn, pea and potato tagine

95–6 Spring lamb meatballs with broad beans and courgettes

98 Yemeni lentil meatballs

100 Stuffed aubergine boats

103–4 Chicken braised in spicy matbucha and cracked wheat pilaf

106 Roasted duck legs with clementines and apricots

108–9 Quails with cannellini bean hummus, pepper and chilli butter

111–12 Feather blade braised with pumpkin, spices and prunes

149–50 Shishbarak

152–53 Celeriac mafrum

168 Rabbit stifado

177–78 Sardines with roasted tomatoes and crispy pitta

225–26 Fish pastilla

228–29 Chicken maklooba

232 Lamb chops with rocket, figs and walnuts

234–35 Royal mansaf

Breakfast (or any time really)

23–4 Green shakshuka

27 Mushroom scrambled eggs

28–9 Borlotti beans on toast with soft-boiled eggs

52 Coconut and lime pancakes with mango

Relishes, sauces and pastes

76 Fig relish

78–9 Walnut tahini

82 Pistachio cream

89 Sesame dressing

221–22 Tahini BBQ sauce

265 Amba relish

266 Amba sauce

272 Chermoula paste

272 Green tahini

273 Shata

274 Pilpelchuma

274 Zehug coriander relish

275 Sweet zehug

Spice mixes

261 Baharat spice mix

263 Ras el hanout spice mix

260 Sweet spice mix

265 Amba spice mix

Cakes, slices and baked desserts

117 Chocolate cloud cake with red and black currants

118 Strawberry ricotta cakes

156 Medjool date, honey and macadamia breakfast loaf

160 Marmalade and dried fruit cake

161 Pistachio and cranberry cake

163–64 Pear and walnut upside-down cake

181–82 Frozen tahini parfait and chocolate sandwich cake

184 Frozen meringue bar with strawberry and lime

186 Baked custard fruit tart

239–40 Tahini cake with lemon and white chocolate

242 Cherry pistachio Bakewell

245–46 Chocolate pecan slice with oranges

Cookies, sweet treats and others

53 Milk chocolate chip cookies with coffee beans

54 White chocolate chip, currant and orange cookies

56 Sumac and vanilla shortbread

114 Lemon and saffron posset

120 Chocolate financiers with coffee cream

154 Honey and spice cookies

248 Marunchinos

250 Peanut and cocoa nib brittle

252 Pistachio, cardamom and rose marzipan

At home

Sarit and Itamar, this is us: middle-aged couple, married plus three. Honey & Co, six years old, was our first-born, our tiny, happy Middle Eastern restaurant on Warren Street; Honey & Spice, three years old, is the little deli we opened across the road from the restaurant, truly the 'sandwich' middle kid, with a slightly split personality between a deli and a homeware heaven; and lastly our baby, Honey & Smoke, two years old, is a big, screaming, all-attention-seeking Middle Eastern grill on Great Portland Street, just five minutes down the road from its siblings.

We moved to London from Israel on Christmas Eve 2004. We knew almost nothing and no one, but we were head-over-heels in love with our new town and hungry for our new beginning. We weren't really sure what our plans were, but we wanted to experience life. We settled in a small flat in Clapham, which we loved. If we ever got lonely, we had each other; and if we got homesick, we headed to our kitchen to recreate some of our childhood flavours, Middle Eastern comfort food – it made us think of friends, family and a life we had left behind, and most of all it made us happy.

When we wanted to make new friends, it was our kitchen we turned to again. Cooking for the people who let us into their lives was an easy way for us to show ourselves, our little story: chopped salad and eggs, cumin and lemon, garlic, olive oil and lamb, and many more things you cannot say with words.

Over the years there have been many meals shared. Lots of people have come, some have stayed and some moved on. There have been birthdays and weddings, births and deaths, silly and serious feuds, moments of great joy. And always there's a table laid, people coming over and us in the kitchen, cooking through good and bad.

As we opened our restaurant, our kitchen at home got abandoned for a while. It was just us two, working all hours of the day. We took everything to work; not only every piece of kitchen kit that could be useful but also the actual dishes we cooked at home – tahini and labneh with little cucumbers, lamb seasoned with plenty of spices, peaches and figs. The food that had brought us together and was a huge part in making new friends was now beginning to bring to our table more and more people: guests at the restaurant and then others, who didn't only want to eat, but also wanted to cook with us, or help us serve our food. As more people joined the team, we could gradually work a bit less, reclaim our home kitchen and really enjoy the precious time we got to spend there. Away from the pressure of restaurant life, we could cook with ease again, play a bit, and be reminded what it is all about – simple food made with care, solely for the pleasure of those you cook for.

Life is complex, but cooking is easy, and something good is guaranteed to happen if you just follow the recipe. Every home, every life, has its anchors and rituals, its own way to come together, its own recipes for happiness. In this book we offer the recipes that make up our home, our lives: from the things we rustle up at the end of a busy day to the grand feasts we spend hours preparing for special occasions. We hope they will serve you as well as they serve us.

11   At home

For us two

Love and cooking. Even the terminology overlaps: things can be raw, tender, pliable, sweet till they've soured. Things are at boiling point, smoking hot, on a knife's edge. Dramas by the kitchen sink abound.

After a week of watching too much American TV, it struck me as odd that we never sit down together for a romantic dinner – coming home to a beautifully set table, soft music, candles. It should be easy for us: we can cook and lay a table, and anyone can light a candle. I can do this, I thought, and it's not often that I think myself capable of doing things I see on American TV.

Something special. I chose an elaborate recipe for Chinese poached fish in a sweet and sour sauce. I got all the ingredients, the candles, the flowers… I should have known I was heading for a fall. Even on American TV the romantic dinner never goes to plan – he comes home to break up with her, she realises she doesn't love him anymore. I had my music on, a glass of wine on the kitchen counter and a recipe that demanded all my attention. Like a low-budget sitcom, my dinner would turn out to be a farce, but for now I was oblivious, even as I took a big gulp of the soy marinade, thinking it was my drink.

I made a new marinade and set the table, arranging the house to the best of my abilities. I don't always see the things that annoy her, so I dimmed the lights to conceal any mess, waiting with the candles till just before she came home from work. Almost done.

My wife was alarmed when she arrived, all her suspicions aroused. What was all this for? What had I done? What was wrong? And she was not the only one alarmed: one of the candles was right beside a dying, shrivelled plant, both under the fire detector, which duly started to blare, drowning the soft music and all thoughts of romance. We ran frantically around in a dark apartment, bumping into each other and the furniture, barking instructions at one another. Turn on the lights! Open the windows! Grabbing whatever we could, we fanned the ceiling in an effort to make that horrible noise stop, while the neighbours came banging at our door – to save us or watch us burn, we are still unsure.

When the sirens had died down and the neighbours had gone home, I was left in a brightly-lit, wind-swept apartment with upturned furniture and an angry wife who was trying to get her heart rate down, calculating in her head how many years of her life she had lost in the last three minutes, thinking perhaps that a shorter life would be a preferable option to the prospect of a long life lived with me.

But still, there was dinner to be had. It looked and smelled glorious, and a bite to eat would surely calm the nerves. I brought out the fish with its glistening sauce on a platter, a pot of fragrant rice. All would be well.

'A bit salty, no?', she says. I agree, but I'm puzzled. There was no salt in the recipe, just a bit of soy sauce and four tablespoons of sugar.

'Did you use the sugar on the shelf or in the drawer?', she asks, guessing the answer and enlightening me: 'The shelf is where we keep the sugar; salt lives in the drawer. You'd know that if you ever did anything around this house'. And with that line, romance left our home that night. Date night for us ended with a bowl of plain rice, a heart racing for all the wrong reasons and a fair bit of anger.

Lessons learned: grand gestures are best avoided, and American TV should be consumed in moderation.

Our romance has always been expressed in more quotidian ways, like spending twelve hours in a kitchen together without killing each other, and still wanting to go home together after that. Coming home exhausted to an empty fridge, wanting to collapse on the floor but still walking into that kitchen, and coming out of it with something tasty and easy for your tired and hungry loved one.

17   For us two

Potato and feta fritters

These fritters are my secret weapon. They have a lot going for them: salty and sweet, crisp and tender, slightly naughty but plenty nice, and they possess the magical ability to make my wife happy. No matter how much laundry is in the basket or if her husband forgot to place the vegetable order for Saturday, these will always put a smile on her face. I don't cook them often – once every year or two. Partly because I hate frying, partly because my wife is quite cheery usually, and partly because I don't want to destroy the magic. But every time I do, it works.

There are few ingredients here, all quite simple, and no wizardry of technique. The success of this dish relies wholly on the attention you pay to the process: the grating, squeezing and gentle mixing; the right temperature for the oil; and the right cooking time. Nothing too taxing, but nothing can be dismissed.

If cooking is part of your life, you'll have similar dishes in your repertoire. Something simple for someone special. If you give these fritters a go – as a pre-dinner snack or as a little meal on its own – I hope they will work the same magic for you, and on the one you love as well.

Makes 10

500g/1lb 2oz Désirée potatoes, peeled and coarsely grated

1 small onion (about 100g/3½oz), peeled and sliced very thinly

½ tsp salt

70g/2½oz/½ cup self-raising flour

100g/3½oz feta, diced in small cubes

1 tbsp picked thyme leaves

freshly ground black pepper, to taste

2 eggs

vegetable oil, for frying

thyme honey, to drizzle

1. Place the grated potatoes and onion slices in a sieve and sprinkle with the salt. Mix well and set aside for about 30 minutes to release some of the liquid. In a separate bowl mix the flour and feta cubes with the picked thyme and a good pinch of black pepper. In another bowl lightly whisk the eggs.

2. Squeeze out all the liquid from the potatoes and onions: the best way is either to pick up small handfuls and squeeze them in your hands over the sink or to place the whole amount in a clean tea towel or cheese cloth, twisting it into a firm ball so that the liquid is wrung out. Add the potatoes and onions to the eggs and mix well. (You can stop at this stage and place the potato mixture in the fridge for a few hours if you are making this ahead of time.)

3. When you are ready to fry the fritters, add the potato mixture to the flour bowl and combine. Heat about 3cm/1¼ inches of vegetable oil in a deep frying pan. Once hot (if you have a thermometer, you want it to reach 170°C/340°F), lower the heat to a steady medium. Scoop little piles (about a tablespoonful) of the potato mix into the hot oil. Fry for 2–3 minutes until dark golden, then flip and fry the other side too. Strain onto a bit of absorbent kitchen paper and then remove to a serving plate. Drizzle generously with the honey and serve hot.

Harira soup

Making a meal when there's nothing in the house? That will probably be our next cookbook. Even though we spend our working days sourcing and cooking some of the best produce available, our kitchen at home is often understocked. Time and again at the end of an arduous day we find ourselves looking hopelessly into the cold depths of our empty fridge. We do, however, try to make sure that our freezer and dry store always have the makings of a few low-effort, high-comfort meals that have saved us more than once. If we have eggs in the house we're lucky. Shakshuka (see page 23) is traditionally a breakfast dish, but we're happy to have it anytime: cook some spices in oil, add tomatoes from a tin (or tomato purée thinned with water), pop some eggs in and bake. That with some toast to dip in it – perfect. Or we make an omelette with tinned crab and soba noodles – sounds weird but it's a real treat. Dried pasta is always there for us and the variations are endless: peas from the freezer with butter and Parmesan is great; tuna, chilli, capers and olive oil is another combo we go back to a lot, and you've not lived until you tried linguini with Marmite and cheese (it's a Nigella recipe and it's delicious). We would be remiss not to mention the mighty fish finger sandwich. So much more than a sandwich, it is a balancing act of bread, fish, crumb and sauce, and when done right, it's one of the most satisfying meals.

The recipe opposite has served us well on many cold, hungry nights. It is a bastardised version of harira, a Moroccan soup with such reviving qualities that it is usually eaten during Ramadan, to break the fast. This version retains the traditional seasoning and hearty spirit of the original soup, but takes some liberties with the ingredients: we sometimes use merguez sausage, but more often than not it's some dried chorizo or a shrivelled salami that makes its way into the pot. When there aren't any vegetables in the house, we make it without, and if there are some that need using up, in they go. Over the years we have made this soup with any and every type of bean that man has tinned. The result is so delicious that it's worth making even when the fridge is fully stocked.

Serves 2 for dinner with some
leftovers, or 4 as a starter

3 tbsp olive oil

2 carrots, peeled and finely diced

2 celery sticks, peeled and
finely diced

1 onion, peeled and finely diced

1 garlic clove, peeled and crushed

2 tsp salt

80g/2¾oz chorizo, merguez or
salami, diced in small cubes

1 cinnamon stick

1 tbsp ras el hanout or baharat
spice mix (see pages 263 and 261)

½ tsp ground turmeric

1 tsp ground cumin

a pinch of chilli flakes
(as large as you like)

1 tin chopped tomatoes
(400g/14oz)

1 litre/1¾ pints/4⅓ cups water

1 tsp sugar

1 tin chickpeas (400g/14oz),
drained and rinsed

1 tin red kidney beans
(400g/14oz) or any other tinned
beans you have in the cupboard,
drained and rinsed

50g/1¾oz/¼–⅓ cup lentils
(any type will do)

50g/1¾oz/½–⅔ cup pasta
(any type will do, but best to use
small shapes)

1. Put the oil, carrots, celery, onion, garlic and one teaspoon of the salt in a large saucepan and set on a medium-low heat. Sweat really slowly, stirring occasionally for about 10 minutes until the vegetables start to soften and stick to the bottom of the pan, then add the chorizo (or merguez or salami) and the cinnamon stick.

2. Mix well and cook for another 5 minutes, then add the rest of the spices and stir well again to toast them a little (about another minute). Now add the tinned tomatoes and the water. Bring to a boil, skim off any fat and then add the second teaspoon of salt and the sugar, followed by the chickpeas, beans and lentils. Bring back to a boil, reduce the heat to minimum and cook slowly for about 10 minutes.

3. Add the pasta and cook for a final 12 minutes. Taste for seasoning and serve. If you are cooking the soup in advance, and reheating later, stop cooking before adding the pasta and add it when you reheat the soup, as the pasta will continue to drink all the liquid and go mushy.

For us two

Green
shakshuka

When I was growing up in Jerusalem you could see them in every
neighbourhood – old ladies in traditional clothes from the villages
nearby, sitting on the pavement with a rug underneath them, bunches
of leaves splayed in front of them, selling the products of their gardens
and field forages. Eggs of different colour and size. Bunches of parsley,
dill and coriander, sandy and fragrant. Mint and other tea herbs:
esoteric things with strange, wonderful flavours – white savory, lemon
geranium, bitter leaves which were used to make a delicious infusion
that was reported to make you sleepy (we called it sheba but it's called
absinthium or wormwood in English). Mustard greens, wild green
chard, spinach, and other vegetal leaves so obscure we didn't even
know their names. We didn't know then about organic or bio-dynamic
vegetables, and foraging then was not the buzzword it is now, but
everyone knew that the stuff these ladies were selling just tasted better.

   We go to the farmers' market on Sundays. Nothing fancy, just good
wholesome meat, some cheese, eggs, bread (which always costs more
than you'd expect), fruit, and vegetables as they should be: beets, carrots
and radishes with dirt and leaves still on them, English spinach with
big leaves and big flavour, leeks and bunches of chard. I always buy too
much. By Thursday all the leaves in the fridge will have to be thrown
away and the eggs will no longer be farm-fresh, so on Wednesday
evening my thrifty wife charges through the fridge and picks them all
out – the tops from carrots, beets and radishes, whatever is left of the
chard and spinach, and all the herbs in the house – before they wilt.
She gives them a good wash and a chop, and stews them all in olive oil.
Once all the leaves are tender and their liquid has gone, the eggs go on
top. Our Wednesday night dinner tastes different every time, but always
makes me think of those women back in their villages, with whatever
leaves and eggs they didn't sell that day, having a similar meal, humble
and delicious.

Green shakshuka

Serves 2 for breakfast, lunch or dinner

3 tbsp olive oil

1 small leek, sliced into rings and washed

100g/3½oz fresh spinach, washed (you can use any green leaf you have here: chard, kale, beets, radish tops, etc.)

1 small bunch of parsley, roughly chopped

1 small bunch of mint, leaves picked and roughly chopped

1 small bunch of dill, roughly chopped

1 garlic clove, peeled and crushed

4 eggs

a few dollops of yogurt (optional)

a sprinkling of sumac (optional)

sea salt and freshly ground black pepper, to taste

1. Heat the olive oil in a frying pan (I use a 22-cm/8¾-inch frying pan) on a medium-high heat. Add the leek and sauté to soften – it will take 3–4 minutes – then start adding the spinach, a large handful at a time. Stir between each addition to wilt it. It may seem as if it will never fit in the pan, but as it wilts there will be hardly any volume left. Finally add the chopped herbs and mix them in to wilt too. The whole process will take about 6–8 minutes, depending on the leaves you are using; just make sure they are soft by the end of it.

2. Remove the frying pan from the stove and season with the crushed garlic and some salt and pepper. You can set this aside until you are ready to eat and the table is set; it will also keep in the fridge until later. You only want to cook the eggs once everyone is at the table, as it is best to eat this while the yolks are still runny.

3. Heat the spinach mixture again and use a spoon to create four little wells in the cooked leaves, one in each quarter. Crack an egg into each well, season the eggs with a touch of salt and pepper and cover the pan. Cook on a low heat until the whites are set but the yolks are still runny – about 3–4 minutes. Serve straight away. You can drizzle with some yogurt and sumac or serve it as is. It's delicious either way.

Saffron carrot soup with a little bit of rice

Serves 2 as a light dinner

25g/1oz butter

2 tbsp olive oil

2 onions (250g/9oz), peeled and finely chopped

3 garlic cloves, peeled and crushed

3 whole cloves

5 whole pimento/allspice berries

a pinch of saffron

2 bay leaves

6 carrots (500g/1lb 2oz), peeled and coarsely grated

2 tsp sea salt

3 tbsp rice (any kind would work here, but I usually use basmati)

¼ tsp freshly ground black pepper

1 litre/1¾ pints/4⅓ cups water

1. Heat the butter and oil in a saucepan on a medium-high heat, then add the onions, garlic, cloves, pimento, saffron and bay leaves and mix to coat well. Reduce the heat to medium-low and sweat the contents of the pan slowly until the onions start to soften and release some liquid (this will take about 5 minutes).

2. Add the grated carrot and one teaspoon of salt, keep the heat on medium and continue sweating the mixture for about 20 minutes, stirring occasionally, until the carrots change colour to an opaque yellow-orange and start to stick to the bottom of the pan. Scrape the base of the pan well and continue cooking for a further 5 minutes.

3. Add the second teaspoon of salt, along with the rice, black pepper and water. Mix well, increase the heat and bring to the boil, skimming any foam that forms on top, then reduce the heat to as low as you can. Simmer very slowly for 30 minutes with the lid semi-covering the pan.

4. Remove from the heat and fish out the whole cloves, pimento and bay leaves. Use a stick blender or transfer to a food processor to blitz to a smooth soup. Taste and adjust the seasoning if needed before serving.

Mushroom scrambled eggs

Serves 2 for a lovely indulgent breakfast or light dinner

25g/1oz butter

1 tbsp olive oil

1 large leek, halved, washed and thickly sliced

2 garlic cloves, peeled and thickly sliced

250g/9oz mixed mushrooms, cut into similar-sized thick slices

½ tsp salt

½ cinnamon stick

1 small bundle of thyme sprigs, tied together with some string

4 eggs

50g/1¾oz/⅔ cup grated Parmesan or pecorino

50ml/1¾fl oz/3½ tbsp milk or cream

freshly ground black pepper, to taste

1. Heat a large frying pan or wok over a medium heat, and melt the butter in the oil. Add the leek, garlic and mushrooms, increase the heat to high and mix well. Then add the salt, cinnamon stick and thyme bundle, and mix well again. Season with plenty of black pepper and stir occasionally for about 10 minutes until the vegetables have coloured and cooked down, and most of the moisture has evaporated. Remove the cinnamon and thyme.

2. In the meantime, whisk the eggs with the cheese and milk or cream and, when you are nearly ready to serve, pour the egg mix into the mushrooms. Allow to set for a couple of seconds and then stir a little. Leave to set for another few seconds and then mix again. Repeat this until the eggs are cooked to the degree you like. I prefer drier eggs but Itamar always likes them softer, so I scoop his out first and give mine another couple of seconds. Serve warm.

Borlotti beans on toast with soft-boiled eggs

Fresh borlotti beans may be hard to come by but they are certainly worth seeking out, if only for their exceptional beauty: the mottled pods range in colour from deep purple to shocking pink and open to reveal pearly white beans with dainty purple specks on them that you could gaze at forever, like pebbles on a beach. Although they look too pretty to cook, they most certainly should be cooked as they are absolutely delicious. The beans sadly lose their beautiful specks in the cooking process but gain a pretty purple hue. They are great at absorbing flavour without conceding their own, but it is their melting, buttery texture that makes another spoonful of these so irresistible. The method suggested here is good for all fresh and dried beans (the dried ones will need overnight soaking) and the result will be so impressive that you really don't need to serve much else with them. Just ladle them onto good toast, making sure to soak the bread with the cooking liquor, and place an egg carefully on top so when you break into it, the yolk runs into the beans to enrich them and doesn't get wasted on the plate. The bean stew will keep for 2–3 days in the fridge once cooked, so can be made ahead.

Serves 2 for a dreamy
breakfast or light dinner

For the bean stew

500g/1lb 2oz shelled fresh borlotti
beans (from 1kg/2lb 4oz whole
pods), or 250g/9oz/1½ cups dried
borlotti beans, soaked overnight in
plenty of cold water, then drained

750ml/1⅓ pints/3¼ cups water

2 large plum tomatoes, cut into
very large pieces

1 head of garlic, just 2–3 mm/
⅛ inch cut off the top to help
reveal the cloves but not to
break the bulb apart

2 bay leaves

1 small bunch of thyme

3 sprigs of sage

100ml/3½fl oz/scant ½ cup
olive oil

1 tsp salt, plus more to taste

For the soft-boiled eggs

4 eggs (you must use cold eggs
from the fridge to get
them perfect)

1 tsp salt

To serve

4 thick slices of sourdough or any
other bread you like, toasted

a sprinkling of sea salt, to taste

1. Bring the beans to the boil in plenty of fresh water, then skim well and cook for 5 minutes. Drain and return them to the same saucepan. Add the measured water along with the tomato chunks, head of garlic and bay leaves. Tie the thyme and sage together with a bit of string and pop them in the pan too.

2. Bring to a steady boil, skimming any foam that comes to the top. Add the olive oil and salt. Simmer very slowly for about 40 minutes until the beans are super-soft (it may take longer if you are using dried beans), then remove from the stove. Remove the garlic head and squeeze all the garlic flesh into the bean stew. Remove the bouquet of thyme and sage, along with any tomato skins that are floating about and the bay leaves (they have all done their jobs). Taste the beans; they may need a touch more salt. The stew will keep well in the fridge for a couple of days.

3. To cook the eggs, boil plenty of water in a small pan, add the teaspoon of salt, prepare a bowl with cold, ice-filled water close by, and set a timer to 6 minutes. Make a tiny little hole at the end of each egg using the sharp tip of a knife, a pin or a metal skewer – this will help with the peeling later. Once the water is at a rapid boil, add your eggs and start your timer. Stir the eggs around for the first minute as this helps centre the yolk (so not vital, but oh so beautiful) then leave to continue cooking for the remaining 5 minutes, before quickly scooping out and popping them into the cold water to stop cooking.

4. Top each slice of toast with a generous helping of hot beans, peel the eggs and place one on each heap of beans, sprinkle with some salt and serve immediately.

Steak fatoush salad with grapes and tomatoes

The days when a meal without meat was not considered a meal are long gone in most homes – certainly in ours. The current mindset of the 'fooderati' has been neatly phrased by Michael Pollan: 'Eat food. Not too much. Mostly plants'. Meat is a treat, a luxury item almost. Going to the butchers' shop is not a chore, it is an indulgence, and here in London we are spoiled with some terrific butchers selling great meat. Frank Godfrey in Islington is where we buy our meat for the restaurant. Not only is the quality superb but the service and commitment make working with them a delight – they will get whatever cut of whatever animal we want, trim it for us in any way we ask and deliver it with a smile.

For our home supplies we go to Moen's in Clapham – the most wonderful shop. They always have great canned and dried goods; they bring in heirloom potatoes, new season garlic and foraged mushrooms; and they have the most wonderfully macabre window displays. For Christmas they hang two big turkey carcasses in full feather, wings and tails splayed to show their impressive plumage. The mums of Clapham are horrified, the kids love it. The meat they sell is superb, especially the beef steaks they so expertly age: full of flavour, tender but not mushy, and if you gasp a little when you come to pay, you know it'll be worth it.

This dish is a good way to stretch a good steak. When we first came to this country and worked on lowly chefs' salaries, this was our treat: a great steak, slices of sourdough cooked in the same pan to absorb as much of its precious flavour, the best tomatoes we could find, and some herbs for interest. Nowadays we can afford a bit more steak, but this dish is still a treat for us. There aren't many dishes that you can bring to the table fifteen minutes after you started cooking, and that are so smart and tasty.

A glorious dinner for the two of us

2 knobs of butter (about 10g/⅓oz each)

2 tbsp olive oil

300g/10½oz aged prime sirloin steak

1 red onion, peeled and sliced in rings

2 thick slices of sourdough bread

1 small bunch of red grapes

3 large tomatoes, sliced

1 small bunch each of parsley and mint, leaves picked

sea salt and freshly ground black pepper, to taste

1. Get everything ready before you start.
2. Heat a large solid-based frying pan over a medium heat, add one knob of butter and the olive oil to the pan. Season your steak generously with salt and black pepper and lay it flat to one side of the frying pan. On the other side of the pan, place the sliced onions.
3. Fry for 3 minutes, moving the onion rings around so they don't burn.
4. Flip the steak and lift up the onions to sit on top of it. Place the two slices of bread in the same frying pan to soak up all the fat and juices, and fry for 2 minutes. Flip the bread (it should be all golden) and lift the steak on top of it. Add the grapes and the second knob of butter. Mix them around and fry for 1 more minute before removing the pan from the heat. Allow the steak to rest on the bread for a few minutes.
5. Slice the steak thinly, rip the bread into chunks and mix with all the remaining ingredients to create the nicest salad ever.

Chicken in plums and sweet spice

We all like our home to be a sanctuary, a haven from our working life, where we can unwind a bit. Perhaps you are more successful at drawing a line between work and home than us. We certainly struggle. Our flat has become an extension of our work, with the constant washing of chef's whites and trousers; our kitchen equipment and store cupboard always in danger of finding their way to work; our dining table always covered with paperwork and recipes scribbled on scraps, waiting to be typed. Even our bedside tables are stacked high with cookbooks and food magazines.

We suspect we are not alone in this predicament. More and more of us are struggling to leave work at work. We've stopped fighting it now and try to make the most of the situation. When we start cooking a tray of this dish before noon so that it is ready for lunchtime customers at our deli, we are hopeful that there'll be a couple of portions left for our dinner at home. It doesn't often happen but when it does, we take our work home with us in a takeaway container and enjoy the fruits of our labour.

An incredible variety of plums are available from late summer until autumn's end, with lots of interesting flavours and colours. You can cook this dish as often as you like between mid-August and the end of October with a different variety every time: greengages are lovely in it, as are sweet mirabelles, spicy damsons… the results will be slightly different but always delicious; a good way to enjoy these seasonal treats. The fruits bake beautifully: the cooking heightens their subtle taste and turns them into a sweet, sour and savoury chutney that is a treat to eat with the roasted chicken, straight from the oven or a few hours later. This dish is incredibly simple to cook – just a mix and bake number – which should leave you with plenty of room to enjoy your hard-earned downtime.

Chicken in plums and sweet spice

Dinner for us and a guest, or just us with leftovers for tomorrow

6–8 skin-on chicken thighs (depending on size)

For the marinade

2 plums (about 80g/3oz), quartered and stones removed

1 tsp whole coriander seeds

1 tsp whole fennel seeds

1 tsp salt

¼ tsp freshly ground black pepper

1 garlic clove, peeled

1 tbsp demerara sugar

3 tbsp red wine vinegar

2 tbsp olive oil

For the roasting tray

2–3 celery sticks, cut into 5-cm/2-inch pieces

1 onion, peeled and cut into wedges

6 garlic cloves, unpeeled

6–8 plums (about 240g/8½oz), quartered and stones removed

1 tbsp demerara sugar

a few sprigs of tarragon, to garnish

sea salt and freshly ground black pepper, to taste

1. Make the marinade by blitzing everything together in a food processor until you have a smooth purée. Pour the marinade over the chicken thighs and mix well to make sure they are evenly coated. Cover and place in the fridge to marinate: a couple of hours will do the trick but you can leave it for up to 24 hours.

2. Heat your oven to 220°C/200°C fan/425°F/gas mark 7. Place the celery, onion, garlic and half the plum quarters in a large roasting tray. Top with the chicken thighs, skin-side up, and pour any remaining marinade over the chicken. Season with some salt and pepper. Roast for 20 minutes, then remove the tray and baste everything well with the juices that have formed at the bottom.

3. Reduce the temperature to 200°C/180°C fan/400°F/gas mark 6 and return the chicken to the oven for a further 10 minutes.

4. Add the remaining plum quarters. Sprinkle with the sugar and roast for a final 10 minutes. Remove from the oven, baste again and garnish with a few tarragon sprigs before serving.

Israeli couscous with tomatoes, feta and lemon

We never for a minute thought, 'It's a good idea to get a bright yellow sofa', but we did it anyway. The one we wanted was grey, a nice solid colour that would blend into the background and not look weird in a couple of years. But the grey one was not in stock. It couldn't be delivered for 8–12 weeks, way too long to wait for anything, and the yellow one was there. She looked so bright and happy, she was ex-display and on sale, and the guy gave us a further discount after a bit of haggling. I guess he thought no one would be stupid enough to buy a bright yellow sofa and took his chance, and as every carpet merchant in Istanbul will tell you: once you haggle, you're committed. We dithered a bit but, not ones to miss a bargain, we took the plunge.

It's not only bright and yellow, it is also rather big. So big, in fact, we couldn't get it through the door. We had to push it through a window.

And so, the living room is now dominated by Big Yellow, as we have come to call her. At first it was hard. We were taken aback every time we walked into the room. We see ourselves as quite optimistic people with relatively sunny dispositions, but that piece of furniture was so bright, slouching there by the wall with her cheerful glow, it was all a bit much.

We got her in the summer and by autumn we had got used to her, but it was in the dark months of winter that she came into her own. When everywhere is grey and miserable, she is there for us – soft and content, slightly scruffy, but still radiating summery vibes like a little private sun.

You can conjure up a bit of summer with this lovely dish – tomatoes, olives, feta and oregano will all transport you immediately to a Grecian island – but you will still get a good dose of the carbs and comfort that are required on this less-than-sunny island of ours; everything you need to cheer you up on a wintry night. You don't need big yellow furniture. But it helps.

We use Israeli couscous here, which is a type of pasta really. You can use Greek orzo or Italian fregola but they will need a bit more water and slightly longer cooking time.

Serves 2 for dinner, with leftovers
for tomorrow's lunch

3 tbsp olive oil

1 onion, peeled and finely diced
(140g/5oz)

2 garlic cloves, peeled and
finely chopped

3 strips of lemon zest
(use a peeler)

4 anchovy fillets in oil (or omit
and use a little more salt)

3 large plum tomatoes,
roughly diced

2 tsp dried oregano

1 tsp sugar

1 tsp sweet paprika

500g/1lb 2oz/3 cups Israeli
couscous (or Greek orzo
or Italian fregola)

1 tbsp tomato purée

1 tsp salt

a generous pinch of freshly
ground black pepper

900ml/1⅔ pints/3¾ cups boiling
water

To garnish (optional)

80g/2¾oz feta, crumbled

¼ lemon, sliced really thinly

1 plum tomato, sliced

2–3 sprigs of basil, leaves picked

1 tbsp olive oil

1. Heat the olive oil in a large frying pan or casserole on a medium heat, then add the diced onion and cook for about 5 minutes, stirring occasionally. Tip in the chopped garlic, lemon strips and anchovy fillets, and continue frying for another 2 minutes. Stir in the diced tomatoes, mixing well, and cook for another 2 minutes before adding the oregano, sugar and paprika. Stir for another minute, then add the Israeli couscous, tomato purée, salt and pepper and stir again until everything is well coated.

2. Add half the boiling water (be careful, it will splatter) and mix well. Allow the couscous to absorb the water fully before adding the second amount. Stir well and cook until completely absorbed.

3. If using, top with the crumbled feta, lemon and tomato slices, and the basil leaves, then drizzle with the olive oil. Serve immediately.

Hedgehog meatballs

No hedgehogs will be harmed during the preparation of these meatballs – we are not sending you to the backyard or the side of the road for ingredients. These get their name from their spiky appearance, and everything you need to make this delicious Persian dish can be found in a local supermarket.

Makes 12–14 meatballs

For the meatballs

400g/14oz/1¾ cups minced beef

200g/7oz/1 cup + 2 tbsp basmati rice, uncooked

2 onions, peeled (240g/8½oz)

1 garlic clove, peeled

1 small bunch of parsley, top leafy part only (about 20g/¾oz)

1 small bunch of mint, top leafy part only (about 20g/¾oz)

1 small bunch of coriander, top leafy part only (about 20g/¾oz)

1 tsp ground coriander

1 tsp ground turmeric, or grate 2cm/¾ inch fresh turmeric root

1 tbsp salt

a sprinkling of white pepper

For the sauce

3 tbsp olive oil

1 onion, peeled and finely diced (120g/4¼oz)

1 leek, thinly sliced and washed

1 garlic, peeled and crushed

1 green chilli, thinly sliced

4 celery sticks, thinly sliced

1 tsp ground turmeric, or grate 2cm/¾ inch fresh turmeric root

2 dried Persian limes (or 3 wide strips of peel from 1 lemon)

2 bay leaves

juice of 1 lemon

1. Place the minced beef and uncooked rice together in a large bowl. Use a food processor to blitz the onions, garlic and fresh herbs together to a paste (or you can chop everything by hand very finely) and add to the meat and rice along with the ground coriander, turmeric, salt and pepper. Mix together until fully combined and then divide into 12–14 balls, each about 80–90g/2¾–3¼oz. Cover and store in the fridge until you are ready to cook.

2. To make the sauce, heat the olive oil in a shallow casserole that is large enough to contain all the meatballs in one layer. Add the onion, leek and garlic and cook on a medium heat until they soften, then add the chilli, celery, turmeric, Persian limes and bay leaves. Mix well and fry for 5 minutes, stirring occasionally, then add 1 litre/1¾ pints/4⅓ cups boiling water.

3. Bring the mixture to the boil and carefully add the meatballs to the liquid. Bring back to the boil and cook uncovered for 5 minutes. Turn the meatballs over in the liquid, then cover and reduce the heat to low. Keep covered and cook for 30 minutes. Open the lid carefully, add the lemon juice, re-cover and cook for the final 10 minutes before serving.

Lamb stew with medjool dates (and sometimes tahini)

It's never worth making a small amount of a stew. Make a large pot to go in the fridge for the week. Serve it on day one with a drizzle of raw tahini paste, mixing it in as you go to get a rich nuttiness. Then the following day, heat and serve it as it is with some rice. Then maybe use it as a sauce for some pasta. It will freeze well too and can be an emergency ready-made meal for a cold winter evening.

A stew for the fridge or freezer, or to serve 6 as a generous dinner

3 tbsp olive oil

1.5kg/3lb 5oz diced lamb shoulder

2 tsp salt, plus more to season

1 tsp freshly ground black pepper

2 onions, peeled and diced

2 carrots, peeled and sliced

4 garlic cloves, peeled and crushed

1 litre/1¾ pints/4⅓ cups water

1 butternut squash, peeled and diced into large cubes

1 tbsp ground cumin

10 medjool dates, pitted and halved

To finish (for the whole amount – reduce if you are only eating some at a time)

5 tbsp raw tahini paste

1 small bunch of parsley, chopped

juice of ½ lemon

1. Heat a large saucepan on a high heat and pour in the olive oil. Mix the diced lamb with the salt and pepper so it is well seasoned, then add it to the pan in batches to brown all over, removing to a bowl on the side once browned. Continue until all the lamb has been seared and set aside.
2. Put the onions, carrots and garlic in the same pan, mix well and cook for about 10 minutes, stirring now and again until the vegetables start to colour and soften. Add the water and bring to the boil.
3. Return the seared lamb (and all the juices that have formed) to the pan, and bring the mixture back to the boil. Reduce the heat to low, half-cover the pan and leave to cook slowly for about 1 hour.
4. Add the diced butternut squash, cumin and halved dates with a sprinkling of extra salt. Continue cooking for another 30–40 minutes or until the meat is very tender.
5. If you are serving the whole amount now, add the finishing touches of tahini paste, parsley and lemon juice, mix well to create a smooth sauce and serve. If you are preparing this in advance, you can stop at the end of step 4 and reheat to serve when needed. The stew will be tasty even without any further additions and will keep for a few days in the fridge.

Tinned tuna cakes

This recipe is inspired by one of our favourite Israeli food writers, Sherry Ansky. We have adapted her original recipe to our kitchen and taste through the years. We allow ourselves this liberty as her excellent writing and recipes are a treasure that aren't widely available in English, so we see it as our duty and privilege to bring this one to you here.

Dinner for us – 8 patties, to be precise

For the fish cakes

1 large potato or 2 small ones (about 180g/6¼oz)

1 small onion (about 100g/3½oz)

1 carrot (about 140g/5oz), peeled and grated

1 tin tuna in oil (160g/5¾oz), drained

1 tbsp small baby capers or chopped larger ones, or even diced cucumber pickles

1 tbsp harissa paste or a little more if you like some heat

½ tsp English mustard powder or 1 tbsp Dijon mustard

2 tsp wholegrain mustard

1 small bunch of parsley, chopped

½ tsp salt

a generous pinch of freshly ground black pepper

For frying

1 egg

70g/2½oz/½ cup plain flour

1 tsp smoked paprika

a pinch of salt

vegetable oil, for frying

1. Place the potato and onion (both whole and unpeeled) in a small pan and cover with plenty of water and a teaspoon of salt. Boil until they are just soft – it should take about 20–25 minutes. Don't be tempted to dice the potato before boiling, as it will retain too much water. Drain the pan and, once you can handle them easily, peel the potato and onion, and cut into small dice. Mix the diced vegetables with all the other ingredients for the fish cakes and make sure they are combined well.

2. Create small rounded cakes – each about 50g/1¾oz. If they are very soft, place them in the fridge for 20 minutes; if they are nice and firm, you can cook them straight away.

3. Lightly beat the egg in a small bowl. Mix the flour, paprika and salt together in a separate bowl. Heat a good amount of oil – about 2cm/¾ inch deep – in a frying pan to around 170°C/340°F. Prepare a plate with some absorbent kitchen paper on it.

4. Toss each cake in the seasoned flour and then dip it into the egg. Carefully pop into the hot oil. Fry until beautifully golden on the bottom, then flip and fry the other side (it should take about 2 minutes each side). If your oil is getting too hot, remove it from the hob for a few seconds and reduce the heat.

5. Serve hot, or at room temperature, or in a pitta on a picnic, along with some yogurt, maybe some sliced vegetables and a squeeze of lemon.

For us two

Arayes

This street snack might be seen as a Middle Eastern burger, as it consists of ground meat and bread, but this is where similarities end. The meat gets some easy Eastern seasoning and is stuffed into a pitta, then this parcel is placed on a hot surface – a grill or a pan. The bread crisps up on the outside, while the inside soaks up all the juices released by the meat as it cooks. We often make a vegetarian version with a thick layer of labneh cheese inside, instead of meat. It may not sound like much – only two ingredients – but is arguably even better than the meaty version. Either way it's a good, quick meal; fast food doesn't have to be junk food. Serve these with a tomato salad and some tahini.

A light meal for 2

For the filling

200g/7oz/scant 1 cup minced beef

1 small onion (100g/3½oz), peeled and coarsely grated

1 garlic clove, peeled and minced

2 tbsp baharat spice mix (see page 261)

2 tsp tomato purée

1 tsp smoked paprika

½ tsp salt

½ tsp baking powder

1 tomato, seeds removed and flesh diced

For the bread

2 pitta breads

1 tbsp olive oil

1. Mix all the filling ingredients together and split into two mounds.
2. Lay each pitta flat and use a knife to slit open halfway to access the pocket in the pitta. Stuff a mound into each pocket and push it all the way in, pressing down to flatten. Brush the exterior of the pittas on both sides with the olive oil.
3. Heat a heavy griddle pan or heavy-based frying pan on a medium-low heat. Place the pittas on the hot surface and press down with a heavy plate or another frying pan. Cook for about 3–4 minutes, then flip and cook on the other side for a further 3 minutes.
4. Remove from the pan and cut each pitta in half. Stand the halves up and put them back on the griddle or pan to colour and cook the cut surface of the filled pitta, and to add a touch of smokiness.
5. Serve with some tahini (try the tahini sauce recipe on page 86, the green version on page 272 or a walnut one on pages 78–9) and some sliced tomatoes.

Tagines

We have an earthenware tagine pot at home. We got it as a gift and it proved to be a very useful one. We used to keep all our change in it, plus coins of different currencies we would one day use again, business cards we would one day call upon, and our spare set of keys – various miscellanea that we didn't want to lose. The conical, tight-fitting lid was perfect for keeping all this debris out of sight. Its pretty silhouette looked so nice on the sideboard. It never entered the kitchen; for our slow-cooked dishes, Moroccan-flavoured or otherwise, we used to use our big, blue enamel pot. We would always get good results.

You begin to understand what a tagine is all about when you find yourself, as we did, on a rooftop in Marrakech at dusk, when the winds from the Atlas turned the hot Sahara day into a surprisingly chilly night. The mint tea in our glasses grew cold in seconds, but the perfumed lamb in the tagine stayed hot enough to burn our tongues long into the night.

A tagine is a genius contraption, perfectly suited to its culture and environment. In a time and place where no one had an oven at home but everyone could light a fire, tagines served as little ovens. The thick clay provides an even distribution of heat; the tight lid keeps the temperature and flavour from escaping; the conical shape traps the evaporating moisture and forces it to drip back down to keep your stew moist; the little knob at the top makes it possible to handle; and, best of all, the bottom bit is not only a cooking vessel, but also a serving dish – a plate you can eat from directly, and one that keeps your food hot. Anything that saves on washing up is great in our book.

So back in London we emptied our tagine and brought it in the kitchen, where it now belongs. A good gift got even better.

They say that an old tagine pot flavours the food. I don't believe this is true. If anything, it's the old hands that have cooked that dish many times which give it that special flavour. They say that food cooked in a tagine tastes different, better. Again, I don't believe this to be true, but if you do end up using a traditional tagine pot to cook and eat the three lovely recipes that follow, then it will give you a first-hand experience – an insight and a connection to a time, place and culture – like nothing else can. Except maybe a delicious dinner on a Marrakech rooftop.

Lamb tagine with runner beans and tomatoes

Dinner for 2, but really easy to scale up (allow one shank per person)

6 garlic cloves, unpeeled

1 red chilli, cut in half lengthways

3 shallots, peeled and halved

2 large lamb shanks

1 tbsp cumin seeds

1 tbsp coriander seeds

1 tbsp fennel seeds

2 tins whole plum tomatoes (400g/14oz)

1 tsp sugar

1 heaped tsp dried oregano

½ lemon, cut into thin slices

1 small bunch of runner beans (about 10–12 pods), cut into 5-cm/2-inch pieces

salt and freshly ground black pepper, to taste

1. Heat your oven to 240°C/220°C fan/475°F/gas mark 9. Place the garlic cloves, chilli and shallots in a tagine base or casserole, and top with the lamb shanks. Season generously with salt and pepper, and place in the centre of the oven to roast uncovered for 30 minutes.

2. Add the whole spices and return to the oven for 3 minutes to toast them lightly, then add the tinned tomatoes, sugar, dried oregano and an extra sprinkling of salt. Cover with a well-fitting tagine or casserole lid, or you can use a sheet of aluminium foil, and return the dish to the oven. Reduce the heat to 200°C/180°C fan/400°F/gas mark 6 and cook for 1 hour.

3. Carefully remove from the oven, baste well with the tomato sauce, then re-cover and return to the oven. Reduce the heat again, to 180°C/160°C fan/350°F/gas mark 4, and cook for a further hour.

4. Remove from the oven, baste again and add the lemon slices and runner beans. Re-cover and return to the oven. Reduce the temperature to 170°C/150°C fan/325°F/gas mark 3–4 this time, and cook for 30 minutes before basting for the last time. Check the amount of liquid in the casserole; if you think it seems a little dry, add half a cup of water but otherwise just baste and return to the oven for the last time. After another 30 minutes the meat should be really soft and tender. Serve with some rice or bread.

Essaouira fish tagine

To marinate the fish

2 sea bream or bass (about 400–600g/14–21oz each), filleted but keep the bones and heads if you are making your own stock

2 tbsp chermoula paste (see page 272)

For quick fish stock (if not using shop-bought)

heads and bones from 2 fish

1 onion, peeled and quartered

1 carrot, peeled and halved lengthways

2 celery sticks

1 tbsp fennel seeds

1 tbsp coriander seeds

For the sauce

2 tbsp tomato purée

2 tbsp chermoula paste (see page 272)

a tiny pinch of saffron

a tiny pinch of ground turmeric

½ tsp salt

a pinch of sugar

500ml/18fl oz/2 cups fish stock

1. Rub the fish fillets with the chermoula paste and keep in the fridge until you are ready to cook them (you can leave them for up to 24 hours).
2. To make the stock, place all the ingredients in a large saucepan with enough water to just cover. Bring to the boil and skim any foam that comes to the top, then reduce the heat to low and simmer for 30 minutes. Strain the stock through a fine sieve.
3. Whisk all the ingredients for the sauce together until well-combined, then pour into your tagine or casserole. Slowly bring to the boil, then reduce the heat and simmer for 10 minutes.
4. Carefully place the fillets of fish into the sauce and push them down so that they are completely covered. Cover the tagine or casserole and cook for 10 minutes on a medium heat before carefully removing the lid. Serve with some couscous.

Prawn, pea and potato tagine

A perfect, quick spring tagine for 2

2 tbsp olive oil

5 large spring onions

2 garlic cloves, peeled and crushed

200g/7oz baby potatoes, peeled and halved, or large potatoes, cubed

30g/1oz preserved lemons, chopped

150g/5¼oz/1 cup shelled peas (if you can get fresh pods, buy 400g/14oz and retain the pods in a large bowl)

a pinch of ground turmeric

a pinch of saffron

1 tsp whole coriander seeds

8 large prawns (shells and heads in tact)

salt and freshly ground black pepper, to taste

1. Place the olive oil in a tagine or heavy-based pan with a well-fitting lid and heat on a medium-low setting. Chop the spring onions. Retain the green parts for later and place the white parts in the pan with the crushed garlic. Sauté for 1 minute, then add the potato halves (or cubes) and a sprinkling of salt. Sauté for about 10 minutes, stirring occasionally and keeping the heat low. Stir in the preserved lemons and half the peas, then add the turmeric, saffron and coriander seeds. Season with another pinch of salt and sauté for another minute.

2. If you have used peas in their pods, boil some water and pour two cups over the empty shells; they will infuse and give the water added flavour. If you don't have any peapods, it is ok — just use boiling water. Add one cup of the water to the tagine. Increase the heat to bring to the boil, then cover and cook for 5 minutes.

3. Open the lid carefully and place the prawns in the liquid, pushing them in between the potatoes and peas. Top with the remaining peas and the green parts of the spring onions, and season well with salt and pepper. If there is not much liquid left, top it up a little with more boiling water (infused, if you have it) so that it just covers the prawns. Replace the lid and cook for 8–10 minutes. The prawns should have turned a deep pink. If they are really large, it may take a couple more minutes, but don't leave them to cook for too long. Serve immediately.

Coconut and lime pancakes with mango

Few things speak of Sunday morning indulgence more than home-made pancakes, and though there is pleasure in cooking for the people you love, in this case we feel it is better to be on the receiving, rather than the giving, end of business. Mixing batter and frying first thing in the morning is not an ideal start to our day of rest, but if you think otherwise you are very welcome to come and live with us. You can make pancakes for us in the mornings; we will do all the other meals and be eternally grateful.

These pancakes are particularly light and pillowy because of the coconut milk used instead of cow's, and the addition of yeast to the batter which makes it more like a crumpet or the Lebanese atayef. Also like atayef, these are drenched in a simple syrup as soon as they are ready, but this one is flavoured with lime rather than orange blossom. Sharp and fresh, it brings the pancakes to life and wakes up the palate. A few slices of mango and/or a dollop of coconut cream or rich yogurt will make this a hero's breakfast, but if you really want to go to town, serve these with a good mango sorbet or your favourite ice cream as dessert at dinnertime instead of breakfast – a much more suitable time to be cooking.

Makes 8 pancakes

For the batter

175g/6oz/scant ¾ cup coconut milk

10g/⅓oz fresh yeast or 1 tsp dried active yeast

2 tbsp sugar

1 egg

150g/5¼oz/1 cup + 2 tbsp plain flour

a pinch of salt

zest of 1 lime

¼ tsp bicarbonate of soda

a little vegetable oil, for frying

To serve

juice of 1 lime

1 tbsp sugar

1 mango, peeled and sliced

1. In a large bowl mix the coconut milk with the yeast and sugar. Set aside for 20 minutes to allow it to start bubbling up.
2. Add the egg and mix well, then fold in the rest of the ingredients until the batter just comes together.
3. Heat a non-stick frying pan on a medium-low setting and use a brush or some kitchen paper to dab a little vegetable oil all over the base of the pan. Use a large spoon to dollop pancake mix into the pan. Fry the pancakes on a nice low heat until large bubbles appear on the surface, then flip them to cook on the other side for about 30 seconds. Remove the pancakes to a warm serving dish, and continue frying until all the batter has been used up.
4. Mix the lime juice and sugar together to create a quick syrup and pour all over the pancakes. Serve with the sliced mango.

Milk chocolate chip cookies with coffee beans

You'd be wise to skip the next few recipes. They are dead easy to make and extraordinarily delicious. The batch is quite big and you can't really halve it (because why would you halve one egg?). The upside is that the dough freezes really well, so when something sweet and homey is in order, nothing is easier then popping one or two cookies in the oven. So easy in fact that you may find the batch disappearing much quicker than you anticipated. Then you'll make another batch and another... it's a slippery slope. Much better to skip these recipes and never know how good these cookies are.

Makes 16 cookies

125g/4½oz butter

220g/7¾oz/1 cup + 2 tbsp dark brown sugar

1 egg

280g/10oz/2 cups + 2 tbsp self-raising flour

¼ tsp salt

150g/5¼oz milk chocolate

25g/1oz crushed coffee beans

½ tsp Turkish coffee powder (optional)

1. Cream the butter with the sugar using a large wooden spoon or an electric mixer with a paddle attachment until it's all creamy, but not too fluffy. Add the egg and beat until fully combined. Add the flour, salt, milk chocolate, crushed coffee beans and coffee powder (if using) and beat together to combine to an even dough.

2. Divide the dough into 16 large balls, each about 50–60g/1¾–2¼oz. Set on a tray and freeze for at least 1 hour. You can make and freeze the dough well in advance to bake when needed (sometimes a cookie is required).

3. Heat your oven to 200°C/180°C fan/400°F/gas mark 6. Once it is up to temperature, remove the cookies from the freezer and place eight at a time on a tray with plenty of space in between them, as they will spread quite a bit. (It is best to bake these from frozen.)

4. Cook in the centre of the oven for 10 minutes. Open the oven and rotate the tray for an even bake, then set a timer for another 5 minutes. The cookies should have spread and turned a light golden colour, but they will still feel soft. Let them set on the tray before serving. Once fully cooled they can be stored in an airtight container.

White chocolate chip, currant and orange cookies

Makes 16 cookies

125g/4½oz soft butter

110g/4oz/½ cup + 1 tbsp light brown sugar

110g/4oz/½ cup + 1½ tbsp caster sugar

zest of 1 orange

1 egg

280g/10oz/2 cups + 2 tbsp self-raising flour

a pinch of salt

150g/5¼oz/generous 1 cup dried currants

150g/5¼oz chopped white chocolate (or use chocolate chips)

1. Use a large wooden spoon or an electric mixer with a paddle attachment to cream the butter with both types of sugar and the orange zest until it is all creamy, but not too white and fluffy as you may lose texture and structure in the baked cookies. Add the egg and beat until fully combined, then add the flour, salt, currants and chopped white chocolate, and mix to an even dough.

2. Divide the dough into 16 large balls, each about 50–60g/1¾–2¼oz. Set on a tray and freeze for at least 1 hour. You can make and freeze the dough well in advance to bake when needed (sometimes a last-minute cookie is essential).

3. Heat your oven to 200°C/180°C fan/400°F/gas mark 6. Once it is up to temperature, remove the cookies from the freezer and place eight at a time on a tray with plenty of space in between them, as they will spread quite a bit. (It is best to bake these from frozen so that the centre stays gooey while the outside has crunch.)

4. Cook in the centre of the oven for 10 minutes. Open the oven and rotate the tray for an even bake, then set a timer for another 5 minutes. The cookies should have spread and turned a light golden colour, but they will still feel soft. Let them set on the tray before serving. Once fully cooled they can be stored in an airtight container.

Sumac and vanilla shortbread

Makes 24–28 shortbreads

240g/8½oz butter, at room temperature

120g/4¼oz/1 cup icing sugar

360g/12¾oz/2¾ cups plain flour

1 vanilla pod, seeds scraped out

½ tsp flaky sea salt

For the coating

2 tbsp sumac

2 tbsp granulated sugar

1. Use a food processor or an electric mixer with a paddle attachment to work the butter, icing sugar, flour, vanilla seeds and salt until the mixture just forms a ball of dough. It takes a while to come together, so don't lose faith. Once it has formed, turn the dough out onto the work surface. Divide into two pieces and shape each one into a log – I prefer to make it rectangular but it is tasty in any shape.
2. Mix the sumac and sugar on the work surface. Roll the log in the sumac-sugar to coat all over, then place in the fridge to set for at least 1 hour (or freeze it until you want to bake them).
3. Heat your oven to 190°C/170°C fan/375°F/gas mark 5. Line two baking trays with baking paper. Use a sharp knife to cut each log into 12–14 slices and place them flat on the trays.
4. Bake for 10–12 minutes until light golden, then remove from the oven. Leave to cool on the tray before eating.

For us two

For friends

I am almost 40. I have been in the world of professional kitchens since I was in my late teens. After 20 years in this profession I can say, with some authority: most of us chefs are weirdos. Each in his or her own way, of course, and I wouldn't go as far as to say we are sociopaths, but there is a definite whiff of socio-something.

Are we socially awkward because we spend all our lives in (mostly basement) kitchens? Or is it the other way around: because we struggle with human interaction, we find ourselves hiding in kitchens? Do we turn to cooking as our means of facing a scary world?

Comfort-eating is a well-known syndrome, but comfort-cooking seems to be less so. It is however, a very real condition, afflicting many. We sufferers tend to become either professional cooks or obsessive home cooks. My wife and I are both, and we seem to be getting worse with the years. We almost dread any social interaction that does not involve the cooking of food, conversation about food or the consumption of food. You will see us at parties – the plump, awkward couple in the corner by the kitchen, talking to the cook, hoping he or she may need a hand and we can show our best selves.

If we do manage to get ourselves into a conversation, it'll probably be about food or cooking. When we are in our element, we can let our guard down a bit and relax. We may not offer sparkling conversation, political or literary insight; what we bring to the table – literally – is food. If the conversation flows and we start to feel even a tiny bit comfortable, we seal the deal with an invitation for dinner. We will plan a lavish feast for you, a meal like you've never had before, with multiple courses, rare ingredients cooked in elaborate ways, a meal to wow and win your heart... but on the day you are supposed to come around, we will have forgotten, or get stuck at work, or have a crisis. Our phone will beep and a note will come up: Dinner at ours tonight at 7pm – Shahar, Patsy... Shit, 2 hours till they arrive.

We'll run home dishevelled, smelling of roast lamb, in a mad dash to arrive before our guests. One of us will stop at the shops (that will mostly be me as I can carry more), trying to find the makings of a decent meal – no rare ingredients tonight, while the other (usually my wife) will run home to pick up socks and debris, trying to make the flat look like a place where grown-ups live. If we are lucky, by 6pm we will both be home; two trained chefs in the place where we belong, with years of experience and a few nifty tricks we picked up on the way, plus a few good dishes that have worked for us many times before.

If all is done and we manage to get in the kitchen 30 minutes before our guests arrive, then they will get a starter; if we only get 20, then it's olives and radishes, some bread or crackers and something to dip them in to accompany our drinks. We will put something in the oven or on the stove as soon as we can, a good smell promising our guests pleasant things to come. They may have to wait a bit before they are served, but we will start to relax into the evening, into the serious and pleasurable task of dinner.

Burning
Aubergines

Younger readers will know that the aubergine emoji has nothing to do with the food of the Middle East. I did not know this and was peppering my messages liberally with them, as most of my communication is on the subject of Middle Eastern cooking, in which this vegetable plays a huge part. I realised how close I was to a lawsuit when I read an article about the over-30s using emojis, which clearly stated, 'Don't even try, you will never get it'.

Our age may prevent us from using the language of the future, but it does mean that we have had enough time on this earth to collect a tremendous number of preparations using aubergine, a vegetable so versatile that we are likely to keep finding more and more tasty new ways with it.

The following three recipes all use the flesh of a burnt aubergine. Choose nice, firm, light aubergines with shiny taut skins. The best for burning are the elongated ones, and it doesn't really matter if they are black, light purple, stripy or white, all will produce a delicious pulp with slight variations.

We do feel that we repeat these instructions far too often, but here we go one more time – these are the three ways you can get smoky aubergine flesh, so you can prepare the following three recipes. A standard aubergine that weighs about 300g/10½oz will produce about 150g/5¼oz of pulp once charred, so if you are using a really large, heavy one, use the same maths to calculate what your yield would be – about half the raw weight.

On a charcoal grill
Just put a couple of whole ones on the BBQ, turning them occasionally until they are charred all over and soft when pressed.

Using a gas burner
Remove the pan support rack and cover the surface of the hob around the burner with aluminium foil. Return the rack and turn the gas flame to high. Place the aubergines over the direct heat and allow each side to burn, using a pair of tongs to turn them to cook all over. They are ready when they collapse in on themselves.

Using your oven on a grill setting (or a separate grill)

Line a tray with aluminium foil (it's best not to use baking paper as it can burn, but you do want to line the tray as the aubergines leak a sticky liquid that is hard to clean off). Pierce each aubergine twice with the tip of the knife to stop it exploding, and place on the tray directly under the grill. Allow them to burn, then turn them over to burn on the other side. When the charred aubergines are completely soft, transfer them to a plate to cool slightly. Once you can handle them, slit and scoop out all the flesh into a bowl with a spoon. Some people prefer to drain them before using, but in most recipes I like to keep the liquid that accumulates, as it is full of wonderful smokiness. Some believe that metal interferes with the flavour and colour of the aubergine flesh and so use a wooden spoon to chop them. We have always used steel knives and think it's fine. Whatever you use, chop the aubergine pulp roughly.

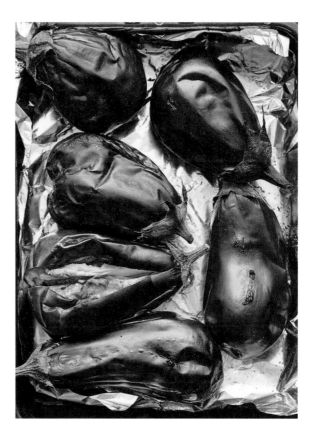

Zaalouk

For 4–6 to share as a mezze dish

2 tbsp olive oil

3 garlic cloves, peeled and finely chopped

a pinch of cayenne pepper

½ tsp freshly ground cumin

½ tsp freshly ground caraway

1 tbsp tomato purée

1 tbsp rose harissa paste

pulp of 3 firm aubergines (about 450g/1lb) – see pages 64–5

juice of ½ lemon

½ tsp sea salt

1. Mix the olive oil with the garlic, cayenne, cumin and caraway in a small saucepan and place on a medium-low heat to warm and infuse the flavours.
2. When the oil smells fragrant and the garlic has softened (making sure not to burn it), add the tomato purée and harissa paste. Fry for 30 seconds, keeping the heat low and stirring constantly. Add the chopped aubergine pulp and mix to combine, then add the lemon juice and salt.
3. Taste to adjust the seasoning before serving.

Silky green aubergine purée

For 4–6 to share as a mezze dish

pulp of 3 firm aubergines (about 450g/1lb) – see pages 64–5

30g/1oz garlic leaves (ramsons) in season or 2 garlic cloves, peeled

1 small bunch of parsley, leaves picked (20g/¾oz)

1 small bunch of coriander, leaves picked (20g/¾oz)

1 tsp salt

200ml/7fl oz/scant 1 cup vegetable oil

1. Place all the ingredients apart from the oil in a food processor and blitz until very smooth. Keep the processor running and add the vegetable oil in a slow, steady stream. The mixture will thicken – a bit like making mayonnaise with no eggs.
2. Adjust the seasoning before serving.

Romanian white aubergine dip

For 4–6 to share as a mezze dish

pulp of 3 firm aubergines (about 450g/1lb) – see pages 64–5

2 garlic cloves, peeled and minced

juice of 1 lemon

½ tsp salt

3 tbsp olive oil

3 tbsp vegetable oil

1. In a large mixing bowl, mix the chopped aubergine pulp and the minced garlic.
2. Add the lemon juice and salt, then pour in the oils, one tablespoon at a time, stirring between additions, until fully combined.

Tuna dip with broccoli, potato and eggs

The Portuguese deli on Atlantic Avenue in Brixton had been there since we came to live in London. We would go there to get olives and chorizo, salt cod and vacuum-packed cooked octopus, and decent Serrano ham for a very decent price. They closed their doors recently, sadly. But as it is said; when one door closes, another one opens. In a terrible blow to our monthly budget, a Spanish importer opened up a shop a few doors down on Atlantic Avenue. They sell excellent produce but it does not come cheap, so we spend most of our earnings on things we cannot resist: cured meat, artisan cheese and tinned fish, especially tuna, which the Spaniards do so well. We use it to make a dish that was introduced to us by Cornelia, our Swiss German friend; a dish that sounds as if it should be Swiss or German but is actually, surprisingly, Italian – vitello tonnato. The idea of slices of cold, poached veal covered in a grey sauce made of tinned tuna sounds off-putting at best, but anyone who's ever tried it knows it works tremendously well, mostly because the sauce is so tasty. We rarely bother with the veal anymore. Very often in our house, dinner consists of boiled greens and small potatoes we get on the way home. We whizz this sauce up from our precious store of tuna while we wait for a pan of salted water to boil.

This is an excellent dish for entertaining, as you can prepare it in advance and simply serve it when your guests arrive.

Enough for 4–8, depending on what else is served

500g/1lb 2oz tenderstem broccoli
500g/1lb 2oz small new potatoes
4 eggs
2 heads of endive
a sprinkling each of sea salt and freshly ground black pepper
a pinch of cayenne pepper, to sprinkle on top (if you like)

For the dipping sauce
1 tin tuna in oil (160g/5¾oz), drained
1 tsp wholegrain mustard
1 tsp smooth Dijon mustard
2 heaped tbsp mayonnaise
2 tbsp yogurt
1 tsp lemon juice
1 tbsp good-quality vinegar

1. To prepare the 'dippers', boil a big pot of water with one tablespoon of salt for each 1 litre/1¾ pints/4⅓ cups of water. Add half the broccoli and blanch for 2½ minutes then quickly remove with some tongs or a large slotted spoon to a large bowl filled with iced water, to chill it. This will help retain the colour and texture. Repeat with the rest of the broccoli. Once that is done, use the same water to boil the potatoes until soft. It takes about 15–20 minutes depending on their size. The best way to check that they are cooked is to insert the tip of a knife into one: it should go in easily. Drain and set aside.
2. In the meantime, boil your eggs by plunging them into salted boiling water for 7 minutes, then immediately drain and pop them into a bowl of icy water too, to halt the cooking.
3. Put all the ingredients for the sauce in a small food processor and whizz until smooth. Transfer to a bowl.
4. Peel and halve the eggs. Quarter the endive, arrange it with the broccoli and potatoes on a lovely plate, and sprinkle with salt and pepper. Serve with a generous bowl of the dipping sauce, sprinkled with the cayenne pepper, if using.

For friends

Baked artichokes with lemony ricotta dip

The Ottoman-era train line from Jerusalem to Jaffa ran through my childhood neighbourhood in Jerusalem. Passenger trains would run a few times a week and the journey took 3½ hours – it is 45 minutes by car, or faster when traffic is good. There's a new train line now, quick and efficient. Last time I was there, the old track had been converted into a promenade, beautifully paved and lined with lovely gardens, but when we were kids, it was quite wild with thick, thorny shrubbery and urban debris. We neighbourhood kids had endless adventures there. It was our favourite place to play, of course. And we loved finding our food there: in the summer, it was prickly pears. The big cactus plants had abundant but very well-guarded fruit; you had to use a stick to detach it from the plant and knock it into a vessel you held in your other hand (usually a rusty old tin we had found). We got quite deft at using two knives to get to the sweet flesh without touching the thorny exterior. In the tail end of winter, it was artichokes: small and grey, each leaf ending in a sharp talon, growing on sinewy, scratchy stalks. More than a bit of blood was shed picking them, but it was all worth it when we had a big pile of artichokes, simply boiled with some lemons. We would pick the leaves, dipping them in salt and scraping the fleshy bit from the end of each one with our teeth, chucking the rest until we had a big pile of leaves in front of us and a tiny, sweet heart covered in choke, that would neatly detach as you pulled the hairs.

The most convivial way to start a meal, bring a tray of these to the table with a big bowl for the leaves, plus the dipping sauce over the page (or just some good olive oil and salt), and see everyone get stuck in with fingers and spoons.

Baked artichokes with lemony ricotta dip

A starter for 4 or light dinner for 2

2 big artichokes or 4 small ones

1 lemon, sliced

a couple of sprigs of thyme

1 head of garlic, separated into cloves but not peeled

250ml/8¾fl oz/generous 1 cup water

250ml/8¾fl oz/generous 1 cup white wine

1 tsp sea salt

1 tsp black peppercorns

2 tbsp olive oil

For the lemony ricotta dipping sauce

1 tub ricotta (about 200g/7oz/ scant 1 cup)

2 preserved lemons, flesh removed and skin finely chopped

½ tsp sweet paprika

a sprinkling of salt and freshly ground black pepper

3 tbsp olive oil

1. Heat the oven to 200°C/180°C fan/400°F/gas mark 6. If your artichokes are large, cut them into quarters; if they are small, cut them in half. A big serrated knife will do the job best. Rub the slices of lemon on the cut surfaces of the artichokes to stop them going black. To make life easier, you can now scoop out the chokes with a teaspoon or the tip of a small knife.

2. If you have an oven-proof, shallow pan with a tight lid, place the artichokes in it, cut-side up and quite snug; if you don't, just use a baking tray. Place the lemon slices, thyme and whole garlic cloves in between the artichokes. Pour the water and the wine on top, and sprinkle with the salt and peppercorns. Finally, drizzle with the olive oil. Cover with the lid, or with aluminium foil, if using a tray.

3. Place in a hot oven and bake for 30–40 minutes, until the leaves just come out as you pull gently.

4. Remove the artichokes from the cooking liquid and serve warm.

5. Mix all the dipping sauce ingredients together and serve with the warm artichokes.

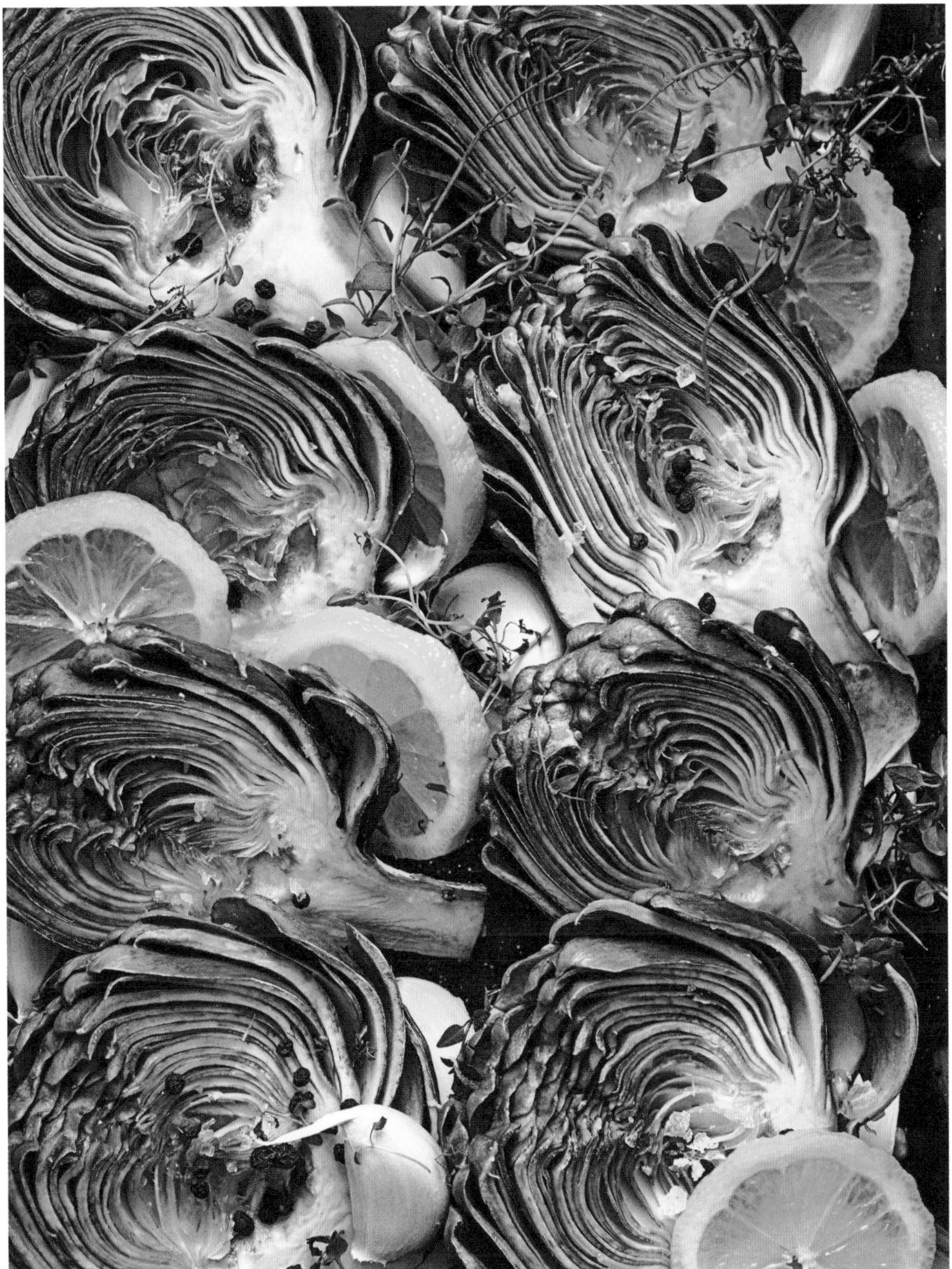

Baked goat's cheese wrapped in walnut pastry with fig relish

This one can be served at the start of a meal or at the end of it, as a very special cheese course – the nutty, crumbly pastry and the oozy, melting cheese inside make for a timeless combo. You can make the relish here, it's easy enough, or use any fruity chutney you like. Change the fruit with the seasons – grapes work well, as do poached pears or quince, but figs, of course, are always the best.

Suitable for 6–8 as a starter or cheese course

2 small goat's cheese rounds (about 100g/3½oz each)

For the pastry casing

70g/2½oz walnuts

70g/2½oz butter

1 tbsp light brown sugar

½ tsp sea salt

140g/5oz/scant 1½ cups spelt flour

1 egg white

1 egg yolk, for egg-washing

For the fig relish

6–8 ripe figs, diced (about 400g/14oz)

80g/2¾oz/6½ tbsp light brown sugar or golden caster sugar

2 bay leaves

a pinch of chilli flakes

1 star anise

60ml/4 tbsp red wine vinegar

To serve (optional)

1 bag rocket, washed in iced water

6–8 fresh figs, quartered

60g/2¼oz roasted walnut halves

a drizzle of olive oil

a sprinkling of sea salt

1. To make the pastry, place the walnuts in a small food processor and blitz to a rough crumb consistency. Add the butter, sugar, salt and flour and blitz till the mixture starts resembling bread crumbs again, then add the egg white and blitz once more until you have a ball of pastry.
2. Remove from the food processor and divide into two balls. Flatten them onto the work surface with the palm of your hand to create two rounds, each about 10cm/4 inches in diameter, more or less. Place one goat's cheese in the centre of each round and, using your hands, lift the pastry up the sides to wrap it. Don't worry if the pastry cracks a little; it is very pliable and you can patch as needed.
3. Lift each one up, and press and smooth the pastry around the cheese to create a solid casing. Pinch off any excess pastry and use the trimmings to create a pattern for the top, if you like (you can create a little leaf by hand or cut out a specific shape). Pat the pastry down all around so you have a clean, sealed finish.
4. Top each parcel with the decoration made from the trimmings and a walnut half (if you wish), then place on a small tray, lined with baking paper, in the fridge to rest for at least 30 minutes before baking. You can leave these in the fridge for a couple of days to bake fresh when your guests arrive.
5. To make the relish, place all the ingredients in a small saucepan with 50ml/1¾fl oz/3½ tbsp of water and set on a high heat. Bring to the boil and stir well. Cook for 5 minutes, stirring occasionally, then reduce the heat to low and cook for a further 8–10 minutes until thick. Remove from the heat.
6. When you are ready to bake, heat your oven to 200°C/180°C fan/400°F/gas mark 6. Add a splash of water and a pinch of salt to the egg yolk you set aside earlier, and mix well to create a thin glaze. Carefully brush this all over the cold pastry (apart from the base), which will give the end result a nice shine. Place in the centre of the oven for about 15–17 minutes to bake to a lovely, light golden colour.
7. Remove the pastry parcels from the oven and place on a serving platter. Add the fresh rocket, cut figs and roasted walnut halves to your platter and drizzle with olive oil and salt. Serve with the relish on the side. This is best eaten while the cheese is still hot and oozy, but we have been known to eat a cold half at midnight, and it still tastes delicious.

Pear and saffron salad
with walnut tahini

Fig season ended suddenly, without any notice. One morning our veg supplier arrived without them, apologetic: he could find none in the market. In a couple of weeks there would be crops coming from South America, but they were not the ones we wanted. No matter that we had three dishes on the menu with figs in them – the season ends when it ends.

But something had to replace them on the menu, so we rummaged through the vegetable delivery van for inspiration. We found a box of pears, small and shapely, light green with just the tiniest blush. Not the juicy, drip-down-your-chin kind, but the crisp, clean-tasting ones – delicious.

We all know what to do when life gives you lemons, but what do you do when things go (literally, for us) pear-shaped? I don't know why the shape of a pear is the shape of things going wrong, maybe because it looks so human. I think it is such a beautiful fruit to look at and to eat, the flavour so subtle and sophisticated, the texture so unique. We should celebrate things that go pear-shaped, surely.

We made this salad, and were so supremely happy with the result that we couldn't give a fig about the morning's mishap – excuse the pun.

The light poaching in saffron syrup, especially if done a day in advance, gives the fruit a brilliant colour, and elegantly matches its taste as well. The bitter leaves work perfectly with both, and nothing needs to be said about the combination of walnuts and pears. It's a classic for a reason. This walnut-tahini sauce is a tasty little number that works well as a dip on its own, or makes a magnificent condiment to serve with roast duck or goose. Roast the walnuts for 8 minutes in the oven at 200°C/180°C fan/400°F/gas mark 6.

A starter for 4 or a side to a
main for 6

For the poached saffron pears

3 pears, peeled

100g/3½oz/½ cup sugar

juice of 1 lemon and 4 wide strips
of peel

5 whole cardamom pods

a large pinch of saffron

½ tsp ground turmeric

For the walnut tahini

120g/4¼oz roasted walnuts

1 garlic clove, peeled

a pinch of chilli flakes

juice of ½ lemon

a generous pinch of sea salt

1 tsp honey

2 tbsp walnut oil or vegetable oil

For the dressing

3 tbsp cooking liquid from the pears

2 tbsp walnut oil or vegetable oil

1 tsp honey

1 tbsp cider vinegar

sea salt and freshly ground black
pepper, to taste

For the salad

1 head of white endive, broken
into leaves

1 small bag of rocket, washed in
iced water

a pinch of chilli flakes (optional)

1. Place all the ingredients for the poached pears in a small pan, add 1 litre/1¾ pints/4⅓ cups of water and bring to the boil. Lower the heat and simmer for 10 minutes. Pears vary in softness so you may need to allow a little more time to simmer. Check them by inserting the tip of a knife into the thickest part of a pear – you want it still to have a wee touch of resistance because they'll continue to cook in the warm liquid even when they are off the heat. If they feel right, simply remove from the heat, cover the pot and allow to cool entirely. If the knife goes in with no resistance at all, carefully lift the pears out of the poaching liquid and into a bowl. Cool the liquid before popping them back in to allow them to infuse and turn to the colour you want.

2. To make the walnut tahini, start by setting aside a handful of walnuts for the salad (about 20–30g/¾–1oz). Put the remaining nuts and the rest of the ingredients for the tahini in a food processor and blitz until they form a thick, slightly chunky paste. Taste for seasoning. It may need a little more salt than you would think.

3. Once you are ready to assemble the salad, choose a pretty, flat serving platter and top with the endive and rocket. Cut the pears into wedges, core and place on top of the salad leaves. Mix all the ingredients for the dressing together. Sprinkle the roasted walnuts over the salad, and then use a teaspoon to dollop everything with the walnut tahini.

4. Drizzle the dressing all over and sprinkle with the chilli flakes (if using) before serving.

Good sides

Too often a recipe will end with instructions like 'serve with a green salad/white rice/boiled potatoes'. Is this laziness on the part of us cookery writers? Not necessarily. If you've taken the trouble to cook something special, you don't really need another showstopper on the table, just a little something to complement, enhance or stretch the food a bit.

We all have our secret weapon side dish: the perfect dressed green salad, roasties that cannot be improved on, your knockout mash. They have served you well through the years and will continue to do so. But it is also true that sometimes the most memorable parts of the meal are the sides – those bits that add interest, texture and context – and sometimes, they should be celebrated.

The following four vegetable recipes are certainly tasty enough to be served on their own as a light meal or a starter. They would stand proud if you were serving a salad spread. They also make great picnic food or lunch box fillings.

But if you have a really good chicken that needs nothing but roasting, or a glorious piece of fish you don't want to overdress, try one of these on the side.

Roasted carrots with pistachio cream, coriander seeds and honey

Sweet, hardy, reliable and always available, the carrot is a true kitchen friend. Here it's getting a touch of lux with nice honey, some spice and lots of pistachios, because sometimes you need to spoil your friends. Use rocket or small spinach leaves if lamb's lettuce or purslane isn't available, and when the season is right, there are a variety of colourful carrots, which will mix things up a bit.

Makes enough for 6–8 as a side or a 4–6 as a starter

For the pistachio cream

100g/3½oz/¾ cup shelled unroasted pistachios

zest of 1 lime

juice of ½ lime

2 tsp orange blossom water

2 tbsp olive oil

a pinch of salt

For the salad

8 carrots – mixed variety would be lovely, if possible

4 tbsp olive oil

1 tsp sea salt

1 tbsp coriander seeds

a pinch of chilli flakes

1 orange, cut into thin wedges with the skin on

juice of 1 orange

2 tbsp honey

1 punnet of lamb's lettuce or, if you can get it, fresh purslane

1. Blitz the pistachios in a small food processor till very smooth, then add the lime zest and juice, orange blossom water, oil and salt, and blitz again. Now add 60ml/4 tbsp of water and mix until combined (you may need a little more water to bring it to a smooth, custard-like texture).
2. Heat your oven to 220°C/200°C fan/425°F/gas mark 7. Peel and cut the carrots into 2-cm/¾-inch slices. Toss them in the olive oil, sea salt, coriander seeds and chilli flakes, then spread on a roasting tray. Place in the oven for 10 minutes, then stir around and return for another 10 minutes.
3. Remove the tray from the oven, add the orange wedges and juice, and drizzle with the honey. Mix well to combine and return to the oven for a final 10 minutes.
4. Place the lamb's lettuce or purslane on a large serving plate, and top with the roasted carrots and orange segments along with all the juice they produced. Dollop with the pistachio cream and serve immediately.

Fennel, kohlrabi, orange and chilli salad

Use kohlrabi if you chance upon it in a farmers' market, as its watery crunch works a dream here. If you can't get hold of kohlrabi, you can make this lovely wintery salad with radishes or crisp apples instead and still get great results.

Makes enough for 6–8 as a side or a 4–6 as a starter

2 fennel bulbs

1 head of kohlrabi

½ tsp salt

juice of ½ lemon

1 red chilli

3 oranges (blood oranges work beautifully here)

1 small bunch of coriander

1 tsp orange blossom water

1 tbsp rice wine vinegar

2 tbsp olive oil

1. Halve the fennel bulbs and remove the core. Lay them flat on a chopping board and slice lengthways as thinly as you can. Place in a large bowl.
2. Peel the kohlrabi, cut it into quarters and then cut these into thin wafer-like slices (you can use a peeler, or a mandolin if you own one). Add the kohlrabi slices to the fennel, sprinkle with the salt and lemon juice, and mix well.
3. Cut the red chilli into thin rounds and add to the bowl. Peel the oranges, slice into rounds and add these to the bowl too. Pick the coriander into sprigs and pop them into ice cold water for 10–15 minutes. Drain and add them to the bowl just before serving.
4. Dress with the orange blossom water, vinegar and olive oil. Mix well and serve.

Fried cauliflower, amba and tahini sauce

Amba is a relish made of fermented sour mangoes and fenugreek, often served with falafel or shawarma. We use sweet mangoes in the recipe on page 266, and we pair our relish with cauliflower, fried to a deep golden brown and doused with loads of tahini. This is one of the most common mezze in the Middle East, after hummus, and is best eaten as close to frying as possible. That said, surprisingly, this recipe also works as a cold salad – just don't expect those cauliflowers to stay crisp.

As a side for 6–8 or a starter for 4

vegetable oil, for frying

1 large head of cauliflower, broken into small florets

2 tsp sea salt

juice of ½ lemon

4 tbsp amba sauce (see page 266)

leaves from a few sprigs of parsley, chopped

a sprinkling of sumac, optional

For the tahini sauce

150g/5¼oz/⅔ cup raw tahini paste

1 small garlic clove, peeled and crushed

1 tbsp lemon juice

160ml/5½fl oz/⅔ cup cold water

¼ tsp salt

1. Heat about 5–6cm/2–2½ inches of vegetable oil in a large skillet for deep-frying. The best way to check it is hot enough is to pop a small floret in the oil as you heat it and wait till it starts to sizzle. Don't put any more cauliflower in the oil until it is properly hot. Cook a small amount at a time, just enough to cover the surface, so that you don't lower the temperature of the oil. Fry until golden all over, stirring occasionally, then lift the florets onto a plate lined with some absorbent kitchen paper.
2. Once you have fried all the florets, sprinkle them with the salt and drizzle with the lemon juice.
3. To make the tahini sauce, combine the tahini paste, garlic and lemon juice in a bowl or a small food processor. Slowly add the cold water, mixing all the time until it comes together in a smooth paste, then add the salt to finish, along with another splash of lemon juice (if needed) to suit your taste.
4. Spread half the tahini sauce on the surface of a large serving plate and top with the fried cauliflower. Drizzle with the rest of the tahini and the amba sauce. Finish with a sprinkling of chopped parsley and sumac (if using).

Brown wheat and broccoli salad with sesame dressing

Brown cracked wheat is one of our favourite ingredients. Flavoursome kernels that are crunchy and yielding at the same time, here they are dotted with greens: avocados, beans and the perennial side vegetable – broccoli. The whole thing is dressed to the nines with a killer sauce that is worth doubling up so you have some leftover for tomorrow's dinner. This dish is so full of textures and flavours that it really doesn't need much else.

A good starter for 4–6, depending on what else is being served

To cook the brown wheat

1 tbsp olive oil

150g/5¼oz/scant 1 cup brown cracked wheat

For the salad

1 large courgette, cut into thick batons

60g/2¼oz green beans, halved

1 head of broccoli, broken into small florets

1 avocado

juice of ½ lemon

For the sesame dressing

2 tbsp white sesame seeds

1 large garlic clove, peeled and crushed

1 small red chilli, deseeded and finely chopped

3-cm/1¼-inch piece of fresh ginger, peeled and finely chopped

100ml/3½fl oz/scant ½ cup olive oil

1 tbsp wholegrain mustard

1 tsp honey

a generous pinch of sea salt

juice of ½ lemon

1. Put the oil for the wheat in a pan along with a generous pinch of salt and 200ml/7fl oz/scant 1 cup of water, and bring to the boil. Add the cracked wheat and bring back to the boil. Stir once, then remove from the heat and cover the pan with a tight-fitting lid or some cling film. Leave to steam for 15 minutes before removing the cover and fluffing the wheat up with a fork.

2. Boil a large pot of water and season with plenty of salt. Prepare a large bowl of iced water alongside, ready to chill the vegetables as soon as they are cooked.

3. Blanch the courgette batons in the boiling water for 3 minutes, then remove with a slotted spoon to the iced water. Next blanch the green beans for 2 minutes, and again remove with a slotted spoon to the iced water. Bring the vegetable water back to the boil and blanch the broccoli for 4 minutes, before draining and placing it in the iced water too (add a little more ice if needed). Let the vegetables continue to cool for 5–6 minutes and then drain in a colander. Peel and slice the avocado, then douse with the lemon juice.

4. Mix the vegetables into the cracked wheat, then transfer to a serving plate. You can do all this in advance and store the undressed salad in the fridge until you are ready to serve.

5. To make the dressing, stir the sesame seeds, crushed garlic, chopped chilli and ginger together in a frying pan over a medium heat for 2–3 minutes to toast slightly. Pour in the olive oil to warm together with the toasted aromatics for a minute, then remove from the heat. Mix in the wholegrain mustard and honey. Add the salt and then the lemon juice. Stir to combine and use to dress the salad just before serving.

Lentil stew with burnt aubergine, eggs, tahini and zehug

The table is laden with little dishes, all humble ingredients but still: tahini, hard-boiled eggs, aubergines, red chilli sauce, green chilli sauce, leaves of parsley, green blades of spring onion, slices of tomatoes and onion, piles of warm, fresh flatbread. A pot is brought in from the kitchen containing fool m'damas – dried broad beans à la Damascus. Cooked simply with cumin and garlic, the consistency is somewhere between a stew, a soup and porridge; the flavour earthy and deep, the beans cooked to yielding submission, melting on the tongue, their broth thick and silky. Everyone around the table gets a ladleful in a bowl, and then dresses it to their taste: tahini on top, always; an egg; as much chilli as you like; a squeeze of lemon for those that need it. You can mix it all together or just let it blend as you eat, keeping every mouthful different, alternating with a bite of tomato, parsley or onion to refresh your palate, occasionally dipping some bread in or saving it to the end to wipe the bowl clean.

This was the weekend breakfast at my aunt's; a traditional workman's breakfast, common from Egypt to Syria, and a ritual we all relished. It may sound bizarre and slightly overwhelming as the first meal of the day, even to Brits who have baked beans as part of their breakfast repertoire. Still, it is one of the best meals you can have, any time of the day. Here we replace the dried broad beans with lovely lentils and give the whole thing a lighter touch. This makes a great spread for a vegetarian dinner, served with all the trimmings and a crusty loaf of bread.

Serves 6

To cook the stew

350g/12⅓oz/2 cups small dark green lentils (like Puy)

1 small red onion, peeled and diced

2 carrots, peeled and thinly sliced

2 celery sticks, peeled and sliced

3 garlic cloves, peeled and halved

1 large plum tomato, quartered

1 small bunch of thyme, tied with some string

1 bay leaf

4 tbsp olive oil

To season the stew after cooking

1 tsp salt

a generous pinch of freshly ground black pepper

1 tbsp ground cumin

2 garlic cloves, peeled and crushed

To serve (optional)

2 aubergines

juice of ½ lemon

a pinch of sea salt

tahini sauce (see page 86)

6 soft-boiled eggs

zehug (see page 274)

shata (see page 273)

3–4 tomatoes, sliced

2–3 spring onions, sliced

1. Place all the ingredients to cook the stew (apart from the olive oil) in a large saucepan and add 1.5 litres/2¾ pints/6½ cups of water. Bring to the boil, skim any foam that may have come to the top and turn down the heat to minimum. Add the olive oil and simmer until the lentils are soft. This will take about 30–40 minutes.

2. Remove from the heat and season with the salt, pepper, ground cumin and garlic. Set aside and allow to infuse for about 20–30 minutes before removing the thyme bundle and bay leaf. You can serve this straight away or reheat it at a later time.

Making a meal of it...

Follow the instructions for burning aubergines on pages 64–65, then season the pulp with the lemon juice and salt. Serve with tahini sauce, soft-boiled eggs, zehug, shata and sliced tomatoes, spring onions and anything else you fancy.

For friends

Spinach, egg and filo pie

Pastry-phobics out there will see this recipe and skip the page. Some people just don't do pies, and I cannot wholeheartedly say I am not one of them, as they can be a bit of a faff. Not this pie: the pastry is shop-bought filo and the filling is very easily put together without much mess. The result will look, smell and taste so good, you'll get huge satisfaction for very little investment.

This is an excellent main for vegetarians and also travels well, so is good for a picnic or as a party contribution.

Makes a 23-cm/9-inch round pie for 8

70g/2½oz butter

1 small packet of filo pastry

For the filling

50g/1¾oz butter

500g/1lb 2oz spinach

1 small bunch of dill, chopped (about 20g/¾oz)

3–4 spring onions, chopped (about 40g/1½oz)

a few sprigs of thyme, leaves picked and chopped (about 2 tsp)

2 tsp dried mint

1 tsp salt

½ tsp freshly ground black pepper

½ tsp ground nutmeg

160g/5¾oz/¾ cup yogurt

50g/1¾oz/6 tbsp plain flour

8 eggs (set 4 aside for the topping)

50g/1¾oz/¾ cup finely grated pecorino

50g/1¾oz feta, crumbled

1. Melt the butter for the filling in a large saucepan. Add the spinach and cover. Cook for 3–4 minutes or until the spinach is all wilted, then remove to a colander to drain the excess liquid. Transfer to a large bowl, add the dill, spring onions, thyme, dried mint, salt, pepper and nutmeg, and mix well. Add the yogurt, flour, four of the eggs, the pecorino and feta, and mix well to combine.
2. Heat the oven to 200°C/180°C fan/400°F/gas mark 6.
3. Melt the butter for the pastry and spread the filo sheets on the work surface. Brush the first sheet with butter and cover with another sheet. Lift these two into the round baking tin, allowing a little overhang. Repeat this process and lay another layer in the tin, slightly overlapping the first. Continue to do this until the entire tin is lined with filo, with pastry overhanging on all sides. You will require about 4–5 double sheets to cover the tin entirely.
4. Fill the tin with the spinach mixture, then fold the filo overhang in to cover the edges of the filling. Don't cover the whole surface; instead scrunch the pastry up at the rim so it will crisp up nicely. Place in the oven for 10 minutes.
5. Carefully remove and crack the remaining four eggs onto the spinach filling, evenly-spaced at 3, 6, 9 and 12 o'clock. They will sink slightly into the spinach. Use the tip of a sharp knife to swirl the yolk into the filling but don't push it in too much. Return to the oven and bake for a further 20 minutes until the spinach mixture is fully set, the eggs are baked and the pastry is crisp all over.

Spring lamb meatballs with broad beans and courgettes

You wouldn't think of broad beans as controversial, but we've certainly found ourselves in many heated debates about them: should the thin membrane be removed before cooking or should it stay on? To peel or not to peel?

For many cooks, peeling broad beans is just something you do, like peeling a banana – you don't eat the skin.

Don't peel, we say. If they are nice and fresh, they'll be delicious. If they are old and mealy, they won't be nice, skin on or off. So many people give this lovely bean a miss because they think it's too much work, which is an incredible shame as broad beans are a celebration of spring, a treat that should be enjoyed throughout the season.

Don't peel, we say. The whole joy of broad beans – that bittersweet taste, that crunch – it's all in the skin. Lose that and you are basically left with something that tastes like a garden pea. If you want that, just get garden peas.

Don't peel. It is so much work, so time consuming. We bought a bag of broad beans once in a farmers' market in south Kensington. We shelled and peeled them on the bus back home to Battersea, where we lived at the time. We got off the bus 45 minutes later with a fistful of beans, a bag full of waste and aching fingers. There are much better ways to spend your precious kitchen time.

If you're still not convinced, you will be once you have tried this recipe. It's a recipe for meatballs, yes, but the broad beans are the stars here: cooked in olive oil, gentle spices and plenty of dill, with leeks and courgettes that melt into the sauce, while the beans, sheltered in their skins, keep their shape and flavour through the cooking, so when you take a spoonful, they roll off the tongue and pleasantly pop in your mouth. You will never peel a broad bean again.

Spring lamb meatballs with broad beans and courgettes

Dinner for 4 (or a greedy 3!)

For the meatballs

1 leek, sliced and washed

1 garlic clove, peeled and crushed

2 tbsp olive oil

250g/9oz/1 cup minced lamb

250g/9oz/1 cup minced beef

1 tbsp each of ground fenugreek and ground coriander

1 tsp ground turmeric

1 tsp table salt

a pinch of freshly ground black pepper

2 tbsp breadcrumbs

1 egg

½ small bunch of dill, chopped (about 10g/⅓oz)

½ small bunch of parsley, leaves picked and chopped (about 10g/⅓oz)

½ tsp baking powder

For the cooking liquid

3 tbsp olive oil

1 large leek, roughly sliced and washed

2 garlic cloves, peeled and halved

2 courgettes, diced

½ tsp table salt

200g/7oz/1½ cups shelled broad beans

2 bay leaves

1 cinnamon stick

½ small bunch of dill, chopped

½ small bunch of parsley, leaves picked and chopped

1. Heat the oven to 220°C/200°C fan/425°F/gas mark 7. In a large bowl mix all the meatball ingredients together until well combined, then shape into 12–14 balls, each about the size of a ping-pong ball. Place on a roasting tray, bake for 12 minutes, then remove from the oven and allow to cool a little.

2. In the meantime, heat the olive oil for the cooking liquid in a large pot and sweat the leeks, garlic and courgettes together for about 5–6 minutes, then sprinkle with the salt and cook for another 2 minutes. Add the broad beans, bay leaves and cinnamon stick, and sauté for a further 5 minutes.

3. Tip in the seared meatballs with any juices that may have formed in the roasting tray. Add 500ml/18fl oz/generous 2 cups of water and bring to the boil. Reduce the heat to minimum, add the chopped herbs and cover the pan. Simmer for 40 minutes, then serve.

Yemeni lentil meatballs

Everyone loves meatballs, and these are always a winner. The addition of lentils makes the texture really pop, and the deceptively simple sauce is full of flavour. We serve them with generous dollops of green tahini (see page 272), marinated cherry tomatoes, and charred pitta bread to soak up all that sauce.

Makes about 18 balls
(enough for 6 for dinner)

For the meatball mix

100g/3½oz/½ cup Puy lentils

1 small onion, peeled and roughly chopped

1 small bunch of coriander, top leafy part only

1 green chilli, halved and seeds removed

2 garlic cloves, peeled

500g/1lb 2oz/2 cups minced beef

500g/1lb 2oz/2 cups minced lamb

1 tbsp ground cumin

1 tsp each ground turmeric, cardamom and fenugreek

½ tsp freshly ground black pepper

1 tbsp salt

To cook the meatballs

3 onions, peeled and sliced

3 bay leaves

To serve (optional)

charred pitta breads (use a grill, toaster or gas burner)

green tahini (see page 272)

a punnet of cherry tomatoes, halved and marinated in some salt, oil and vinegar

leaves from a few sprigs of coriander (optional)

1. Boil the lentils in plenty of water until they are soft – this will take about 30 minutes. Drain and set aside to cool.
2. In a food processor (or using a fine grater), mince the onion, coriander, chilli and garlic together to a paste and transfer to a large mixing bowl. Add the beef and lamb mince to the bowl with all the remaining meatball ingredients. Mix everything together really well until thoroughly combined. Portion the mixture into 18 balls, each about 80g/2¾oz.
3. Heat your oven to 220°C/200°C fan/425°F/gas mark 7. To cook the meatballs, place the sliced onions and bay leaves in a large, deep roasting tray or casserole, and top with the meatballs in one layer.
4. Roast uncovered for 15 minutes. Remove from the oven, and carefully add enough water to cover the onions, but reaching no more than halfway up the meatballs. Return to the oven and roast for 15 minutes uncovered. Remove from the oven and carefully flip all the balls into the liquid. Cover the tray with aluminium foil or a lid, reduce the heat to 200°C/180°C fan/400°F/gas mark 6 and cook for a further hour.
5. Serve with warm pitta breads, green tahini, halved cherry tomatoes and coriander if desired.

Stuffed aubergine boats

Serves 4 as a main or 8 as part of a
larger spread of dishes

For roasting the boats

4 small aubergines

4 tbsp olive oil

1 garlic clove, peeled and crushed

a generous sprinkling each of salt
and pepper

For the filling

1 large onion (about 140g/5oz),
peeled and finely diced

3 tbsp olive oil

400g/14oz/1¾ cups minced lamb

1 tsp salt

1 tbsp baharat spice mix
(see page 261)

1 tsp ground cinnamon

½ tsp ground turmeric

2 tsp tomato purée

For the topping

10–12 cherry tomatoes, halved

80g/2¾oz feta, crumbled

leaves from a few sprigs
of parsley, chopped

1. Heat your oven to 220°C/200°C fan/425°F/gas mark 7.
2. Halve the aubergines lengthways. Use a small knife to score the flesh of the aubergines in a criss-cross pattern, taking care not to cut through the skin. Mix the olive oil with the garlic, salt and pepper, and brush very generously all over the flesh of the aubergines. Place on a tray in the oven and roast, cut-side up, for 15–20 minutes or until the flesh is beautifully golden and feels soft when pressed. Remove from the oven.
3. In the meantime, place the diced onion and oil in a frying pan over a high heat and cook until golden. Add the minced lamb and salt, keep the heat high and use a spoon to break the meat into little pieces so that it starts to brown. Mix in the spices and cook for 3–4 minutes. Stir in the tomato purée and 4 tbsp of water, and continue to stir while it cooks for a further 3 minutes.
4. Spoon the mince onto the roasted aubergine boats, using up all the mixture, and spread to cover the cut surfaces. Top with the tomato halves and feta, and return to the oven for 10 minutes. Remove and sprinkle with the chopped parsley just before serving.

101   For friends

For friends

Chicken braised in spicy matbucha and cracked wheat pilaf

Why is it that every pleasure has a price? At the end of every meal there will inevitably be a pile of dishes and a messy kitchen that someone will have to deal with. It is a long-standing truth that in a professional kitchen you can do without half the chefs, but you can't do without the kitchen porter.

At home, sadly, we don't have a kitchen porter, but we do have a dishwasher, and everything we have in the kitchen is considered by us to be dishwasher-safe (one exception: our beautiful, handmade chef's knives). We often wonder how much cooking and entertaining would be done in our house if this wonderful machine didn't exist; very little, is the probable answer.

We still try to keep the mess to a minimum, and are always on the lookout for more one-pot meals. They make great kitchen sense to us: not only do you save on dishes, you also gain on taste, as all the components of your meal get to mingle, each one flavouring the others.

If, like us, you are looking to add to your one-pot-wonders repertoire, do try this one for size. Tomatoes, peppers and lemons make up a simple, delicious sauce called matbucha. The chicken thighs take on these flavours and add to the sauce a savoury richness. Cracked wheat kernels absorb all of this as they cook, giving the dish texture and substance. This one pot contains a wholesome, balanced meal – hearty and satisfying without being heavy or bland, full of different textures, and incredibly tasty. Saving on dishes is the least of your reasons to make it; that is simply an added bonus.

Chicken braised in spicy matbucha and cracked wheat pilaf

Dinner for 4 (or a greedy 3!)

1kg/2lb 4oz skin-on chicken thighs

2 tsp salt

½ lemon, quartered and sliced very thinly

1 red chilli, sliced thinly

2 garlic cloves, peeled and sliced

1 long red pepper, cut into thick rings

3 plum tomatoes, cut into thick slices

2 tsp sugar

20 cherry tomatoes (any type will do – but a mix is really nice)

1 small bunch of coriander, roughly chopped

200g/7oz/generous 1 cup coarse cracked wheat

1. Place the chicken thighs skin-side down in a large saucepan or sauté pan and season with one teaspoon of salt. Put the pan over a low heat and allow the fat to render out and the skin to crisp up; it will take about 15–20 minutes. Flip the thighs over and cook for 5 minutes on the other side, then carefully lift them onto a plate, leaving all the fat produced in the pan on the heat. Add the lemon slices, chilli and garlic, and sauté till a strong aroma of lemons comes from the pan. This will take about 3 minutes.

2. Increase the heat to medium-high and add the pepper rings. Sauté for 3 minutes, stirring all the time, then add the plum tomato slices. Season with the second teaspoon of salt and the sugar, and mix well. Cook for about 5 minutes, or until the tomato slices start to fall apart and create a sauce.

3. Return the chicken thighs to the pan, skin-side up, add the whole cherry tomatoes, sprinkle the chopped coriander on top and finally add 100ml/3½fl oz/scant ½ cup of water. Reduce the heat to a minimum, cover and simmer for 20 minutes, then remove the lid. Stir a little to make sure nothing is catching on the bottom and place the lid back on, but this time don't close it entirely to allow some steam to escape. Simmer very slowly for another 15 minutes.

4. You can eat the dish just as it is, if you wish, but the best thing to do is to sprinkle the cracked wheat into the pot, stir a little and bring it back to the boil. Then re-cover with the lid, remove from the heat and set aside for 15 minutes while the wheat slowly cooks. Serve, all in one.

For friends

Roasted duck legs with clementines and apricots

This should be the centrepiece for your next Christmas meal, it looks so festive and wintery. The apricots will soak up all the lovely duck juices, the skin will crisp and the whole thing will make you want to snuggle by the fire.

Don't be intimidated by duck. This is the simplest thing to cook and really excellent for entertaining as it will not dry out, and can also be made in advance and re-heated to serve. The only thing to take into account with this recipe is that the duck legs need to be salted before cooking: a day ahead, if you can, or at least 6 hours as a minimum.

Dinner for 6–8

8 duck legs

For the salt rub

30g/1oz/2 tbsp table salt

1 tsp ground cinnamon

1 tsp ground coriander

1 tsp freshly ground black pepper

1 tsp ground ginger

For roasting

2 onions, peeled and cut into wedges

2 clementines, quartered

150g/5¼oz/1 cup dried apricots

2 bay leaves

2 star anise

1. Mix the salt rub ingredients together and sprinkle over both sides of the duck legs. Wrap in cling film and place in the fridge for at least 6 hours, but ideally about 24 hours.

2. Heat your oven to 220°C/200°C fan/425°F/gas mark 7 and place the duck legs in one layer in a deep roasting tray. Roast in the oven for about 20–25 minutes or until the skin starts to colour. Carefully drain off the fat (you can keep it to roast some potatoes on another day – it lasts for ages in the fridge).

3. Add the onion wedges and clementines to the tray, and return to the oven for another 15 minutes. Remove the tray again, add the apricots, bay leaves and star anise, and then pour over enough water to reach just halfway up the duck legs (you may need a little more or a little less than 600ml/21fl oz/generous 2½ cups, depending on the size of your tray).

4. Reduce the oven temperature to 180°C/160°C fan/350°F/gas mark 4. Cover the tray, return to the oven and cook for another 40 minutes. Remove the cover and check the liquid level – it should still reach about halfway up the legs. Baste all over, re-cover and return to the oven for another 30 minutes.

5. Remove the cover, baste again and return to the oven for 15 minutes, before basting one last time. Push any apricots into the liquid so that they don't burn, then cook for a final 15 minutes to finish crisping up the skin.

Quails with cannellini bean hummus, pepper and chilli butter

Quail for dinner is always a good idea, at least it is in our book, and we are not alone. When the Israelites were crossing the Sinai desert, they were missing the fleshpots of Egypt. The Lord heard their grumbling and came through with the goods. This from the book of Exodus:

'And it came to pass, that at even the quails came up, and covered the camp: and in the morning the dew lay round about the host.'

Which means quail for dinner and dew for breakfast; a diet prescribed by the Lord himself.

As this little bird migrates from its feeding grounds in Africa to breed in Europe, massive flocks pass through the Middle East. For generations, and still to this day, locals set up nets to catch them in huge abundance. One can easily imagine evening feasts under the starry desert sky, the day's catch cooking on a gentle fire. If this was perceived as divine blessing back in the day, we are not ones to argue, and if this vision of desert Arcadia gets your taste buds going, give this dish a go. The bird's subtle meaty flavour is complemented nicely by the sweet spices; the buttery pepper relish adds richness and a sweet note; and the bean purée is a smooth, earthy, very satisfying bed for it all.

In this recipe the bird is cooked on the bone, as it keeps it juicy and enhances the flavour. You will need to use your hands to get all the meat off, and this is the way to eat; it is finger-lickin' good, as a famous poultry purveyor puts it. If you are serving these at a meal where knife and fork are mandatory, ask a kindly butcher to debone them for you.

Dinner for 4

For the quails

6 quails

3 tbsp plain flour

3 tbsp cornflour

1 tsp each ground cinnamon,
nutmeg, cumin, coriander
and paprika

2 tsp salt

vegetable oil, for frying

For the bean hummus

1 tin cannellini beans
(400g/14oz/1⅓ cups)

1 garlic clove, peeled

3 tbsp olive oil

a generous sprinkling of salt

For the pepper and chilli butter

1 long red Romano pepper
or 1 red bell pepper

2 garlic cloves, peeled

50g/1¾oz butter

½ tsp chilli flakes

a pinch of salt

1 small bunch of parsley, leaves
picked and chopped

1. Use a pair of strong scissors and hold the quail with its back bone facing you. Use the scissors to cut along one side of the back bone, then the other side, so you can remove the spine entirely. Then lay the bird on a chopping board and using a large knife to cut through the breast bone, top to tail, so you end up with two halves. Repeat with the other birds (three halves per person should be sufficient). Set in the fridge until you are ready to cook. Mix all the flours, spices and salt together, ready for frying.

2. To make the bean hummus, drain the cannellini beans and pour over a couple of cups of boiling water to wash off any tinned flavour. Place the garlic in a small food processor and blitz, then add the beans and 50ml/¾fl oz/3½ tbsp of boiling water (to help them to purée smoothly) and blitz again. Add the olive oil and a pinch of salt, and blitz everything to a smooth paste.

3. To make the pepper and chilli butter, halve the pepper, remove the stem and seeds, and cut into the tiniest dice you can manage. Chop the garlic cloves to the same size. Place the pepper and garlic in a frying pan with the butter on a low heat. This is a semi-confit, so low and slow is key here. Let the redness start to seep from the peppers into the butter (it will take 10–12 minutes), then add the chilli flakes and salt, and cook for another 2 minutes until the peppers soften. Once they have, remove from the heat and add the chopped parsley.

4. To cook the quails, heat a good layer of vegetable oil – about 1cm/ ½ inch deep – in a large frying pan. Mix the quails with the seasoned flour so that they are well coated. When the oil is hot, carefully place the quail in the pan breast-side down. Allow to colour for 2–3 minutes before flipping and frying the other side for 2–3 minutes. Lift onto a plate lined with some absorbent kitchen paper to drain any excess oil. You may have to do this in a couple of batches.

5. Smear the bean hummus on your serving plate, top with the quails and drizzle all over with the pepper butter.

Feather blade braised with pumpkin, spices and prunes

The geographic position of Jerusalem, a city on a hill, set high above the desert around it, makes its winters relatively cold. This, along with the ban on cooking on the Sabbath, has led to a fondness for slow-cooked, cold-weather food. Not exactly typical of a very hot country. The Sephardi Jewish community, that has lived in this city for centuries, has a wide repertoire of dishes that are placed in a low-temperature oven on Friday afternoon to be taken out for lunch on the Sabbath, a day when even the cook gets to rest, while still providing glorious food. The famous sofrito is one such dish, and Jerusalem 'cholent' – pulses, potatoes and meat cooked overnight to soft, delicious submission – is another. There isn't a direct translation to English for this cooking method, although pot-roasting is not a bad approximation. It is something between a braise and a roast. A 'broast' perhaps? (We're putting it out there, to see if it'll catch on.) Whatever you want to call it, it's a delicious way of cooking meat.

This dish is another one of those. Beef with prunes is a classic combination, and the two really work well together. The delicate spicing sort of melts into the background, and the pumpkin, with its long strands and sweetness, brings the whole thing home.

Feather blade is a cut worth knowing and is ideal for this kind of treatment. The long muscle hides a layer of unctuous collagen, which will keep the meat from drying out, as well as giving the sauce a nice gloss and an incredible richness, which make the trip to the butchers' really worthwhile.

Feather blade braised with pumpkin, spices and prunes

Makes dinner for 6

1 whole feather blade steak (about 1.5kg/3lb 5oz) or short ribs

1 tsp salt

4 tbsp olive oil

1.5kg/3lb 5oz pumpkin, cut into wedges – I prefer to keep the skin on

1 red or green chilli, sliced in half lengthways – keep the seeds in if you like a spicy finish or remove for a lighter touch

2 red onions, peeled and quartered

1 head of garlic, cut in half to expose the cloves

3 bay leaves

1 cinnamon stick

1 tsp whole black peppercorns

3 whole cloves

10 whole pimento/allspice berries or 1 tsp ground pimento/allspice

a pinch of saffron threads or 1 tsp ground turmeric

200g/7oz/1½ cups prunes (you will use half to cook and half to finish)

1 glass of red wine (and 1 for you – the bottle is open already, so why not?)

1 tin chopped tomatoes (400g/14oz)

500ml/18fl oz/2 cups stock or water

1. Pull the meat out of the fridge about 30–60 minutes before you start cooking. Rub the salt all over the beef and, if you don't have a large enough pot to cook it whole, cut it in two so that it will go in.

2. Heat two tablespoons of the oil in the pot over a high heat, and fry the pumpkin wedges until they colour, then flip and colour on the other side too. Remove to a plate on the side. Now put the remaining two tablespoons of oil in the pot and pop the beef in to brown all over, turning it once the underneath goes a beautiful, dark-golden colour. Remove the meat to a plate and put the chilli, onions and garlic in the same pot to colour too for 4–5 minutes.

3. Return the beef to the pan, keeping it on the heat, and add the bay leaves, all the spices, half the seared pumpkin wedges (retaining half for later), half the prunes and the red wine. Cook for 2 minutes, then add the chopped tomatoes, and finally the stock or water. Bring to the boil, reduce the heat to low, skim and cover.

4. You can now cook it on a low heat on the stove for the next 2 hours, basting and stirring it around every 20 minutes to make sure nothing is sticking to the base or – simpler still – pop the whole pot in the oven at 180°C/160°C fan/350°F/gas mark 4 and set a timer for 1 hour. After that first hour, remove the pan from the oven, baste the meat, and return it to the oven for another hour.

5. Carefully lift the meat on to a plate, strain all the cooking liquid into a bowl and discard the pulp in the sieve. Return the strained liquid to the pot and place the meat back in too (if you wish, you can slice the meat before returning it). Add the remaining wedges of pumpkin and the remaining prunes (previously set aside), cover and either cook for the last 30 minutes before serving now, or set aside to reheat for the final 30 minutes and serve later.

For friends

Lemon and saffron posset

A good dessert for those who don't make dessert. You won't need to scour the markets for obscure ingredients or special equipment. You won't need to clear the afternoon. In fact, this one doesn't even require an oven, only a hob, a pan and some glasses to pour it in. Sharp, creamy, cool and fresh; as easy on the eye as it is on the tongue. A really good finish to a big meal.

To make 6 small possets or
4 larger portions

For the possets

240ml/8½fl oz/1 cup double cream

1 small pinch of saffron strands

80g/2¾oz/6½ tbsp sugar

zest of 1 lemon

40ml/8 tsp lemon juice
(1 juicy lemon should suffice)

For the macerated raspberries

30ml/2 tbsp boiling water

30g/1oz/2½ tbsp caster sugar

1 tsp rose water (optional)

1 punnet raspberries

1. Put the glasses on a small tray (one that will fit in the fridge), ready to be filled as soon as the cream is prepared.
2. Place the cream, saffron, sugar and zest in a small saucepan on a medium-low heat and bring to the boil, stirring occasionally. Once the cream has just started boiling, reduce the heat to very low and stir around while counting to 20 really slowly. Remove from the heat and pour in the lemon juice in a steady stream, stirring all the time. Quickly pour the posset into the glasses. Carefully lift the tray into the fridge and leave to set firm (it will need at least 2 hours to chill fully).
3. While you are waiting, pour the boiling water over the sugar in a bowl. Mix to dissolve entirely, then add the rose water (if using). Allow to cool a little, then add the raspberries and gently swirl the bowl so that the fruit is coated.
4. When you are ready to serve, top each posset with a few macerated raspberries and a bit of the syrup.

Chocolate cloud cake with red and black currants

To fill an 18-cm/7-inch cake tin, lined with a large circle of baking paper

For the filling and topping

200g/7oz/1 cup sugar

400g/14oz/3 cups red and black currants (either colour or a mix)

1 cinnamon stick

For the chocolate cloud sponge

3 eggs, separated

130g/4½oz/⅔ cup dark brown sugar

200g/7oz/scant 1 cup double cream

60g/2¼oz/scant ½ cup plain flour

40g/1½oz/scant ½ cup cocoa powder

1 tsp ground cinnamon

a pinch of salt

60g/2¼oz dark bitter chocolate, finely chopped

The combination of chocolate and fruit is a tricky area, but careful judgment can yield delicious results. Be picky about the chocolate you use here, as you'll need the slight acidity and fruity notes of good-quality bitter chocolate to echo and complement the unique flavour and astringent tang of the currants.

1. Set a frying pan on the hob on a high heat, sprinkle in the sugar for the filling, and stir until it has all dissolved and turned a light caramel colour. Add the red and black currants and the stick of cinnamon and mix. Don't worry if the sugar seizes a little around the fruit – just continue stirring until it dissolves again, then remove from the heat and allow to rest while you make the sponge.

2. Heat your oven to 190°C/170°C fan/375°F/gas mark 5. Prepare your tin by lining it with a large circle of baking paper that you push into the tin, allowing for at least 2cm/¾ inch to stand up higher than the sides of the tin.

3. Whisk the egg whites in a bowl with 80g/2¾oz/6½ tbsp of the brown sugar. In a separate bowl, mix all the remaining cake ingredients (including the egg yolks and the rest of the brown sugar) until well combined. Fold the two mixes together, trying to keep as much air in the batter as possible.

4. Spoon half the cake mixture into the paper-lined tin and sprinkle with three tablespoons of the cooked fruit. Top with the rest of the cake batter. Place in the centre of the oven and bake for 20 minutes, then rotate the cake tin in the oven. Leave to bake for another 10–14 minutes, after which it should feel like touching a light cloud: it will have a little bounce but still be soft.

5. Remove the cake from the oven and allow to cool in the tin for at least 15 minutes. It will sink a little in the centre but that is part of the charm, and also where you put the rest of the fruit and some of the cooking liquid before serving.

Strawberry ricotta cakes

There should be a word to describe the way the soft texture of this cake matches the flavour of the vanilla, strawberries and almonds in it. But that word doesn't exist, so the only way to know how incredibly good this cake tastes is to go into the kitchen and make it. If you come up with a word for it, drop us a line.

For the best results, pull all the cake ingredients out of the fridge about an hour before you start. It will make your baked cakes fluffier and tastier.

Makes 6 small, 9-cm/3½-inch individual cakes, or you can use a 22-cm/8¾-inch round tin for a single large cake

115g/4oz butter

125g/4½oz/generous ⅔ cup caster sugar

3 eggs, separated

2 tbsp cornflour or potato flour

175g/6oz/1¼ cups ground almonds

200g/7oz/scant 1 cup ricotta

1 vanilla pod, seeds scraped out

1 lemon zest

a pinch of salt

400g/14oz/4 cups strawberries

2 tbsp vanilla sugar (made from mixing sugar with the empty vanilla pod)

1. Heat your oven to 190°C/170°C fan/375°F/gas mark 5. Line the cake tins with baking paper (we like to use a circle of baking paper pushed into each tin).

2. Use a large flat spoon or a mixer with a paddle attachment to cream the butter and the sugar together until fluffy and creamy. Slowly add the egg yolks, one at a time, and beat until smooth. Add the cornflour, ground almonds, ricotta, seeds from the vanilla pod, lemon zest and salt, and mix well to form a smooth batter.

3. Whisk the egg whites to soft peaks and gently fold into the cake batter till well combined. Transfer the batter into your pre-lined tins – about 120g/4¼oz in each.

4. Remove the green stems from the strawberries and, depending on their size, cut into halves or quarters. Arrange them in a formation on top of each cake and sprinkle with the vanilla sugar. Place the tins on a tray in the centre of the oven for 15 minutes, then rotate the tray and bake for a further 10 minutes before serving.

5. These cakes can be served warm straight from the oven or kept in the fridge for up to 2 days. Bring back up to room temperature to serve.

Chocolate financiers with coffee cream

To make 12 shallow muffins

For the coffee cream
(best made the evening before,
if possible)

180g/6¼oz/¾ cup double cream

25g/1oz crushed coffee beans
(smash the whole beans to
crack them)

1 whole star anise

1 tsp sugar

For the chocolate financiers

65g/2¼oz/⅓ cup
ground almonds

1 tsp ground star anise (we use a
little coffee grinder)

1 tsp flaky sea salt (try to keep the
flakes large and don't use table
salt if possible – but if that is the
only salt you have, a pinch will do)

1 tbsp cocoa powder

40g/1½oz/generous ¼ cup
plain flour

100g/3½oz/scant ¾ cup
icing sugar

90g/3¼oz butter

1 tbsp honey

100g/3½oz 70% cocoa dark
chocolate, broken or chopped

90g/3¼oz egg whites
(from about 3 eggs)

This is a grown-up, quite sophisticated dessert. Serve it with a glass of good, cold milk if you want to shave some of the years off.

1. Mix all the ingredients for the coffee cream together in a small pan and place on the stove over the lowest heat you can. Allow to come slowly to the boil, stirring every 2 minutes to make sure the cream doesn't catch on the bottom (don't mix too much in case you split the cream). It should take about 10–12 minutes to come to the boil. If it is boiling faster than this, your heat may be too high, in which case remove the pan from the heat for a minute to cool before returning it.
2. After the cream mixture has come to the boil, remove from the heat and set aside to infuse for 30–40 minutes, then strain through a fine sieve and transfer to your serving bowl. Cover and leave to set in the fridge overnight to a beautiful, thick, clotted cream-like consistency.
3. Mix all the dry ingredients for the chocolate financiers together in a bowl. Place the butter in a small pan on the hob over a high heat to melt entirely. Allow bubbles to start forming and let the butter brown slightly (this is a classic French method that adds a really rich flavour and is worth trying), then remove from the heat. Add the honey and chocolate, and stir together to a smooth texture.
4. Mix the egg whites into the dry ingredients and then fold in the butter-chocolate mixture. Leave to rest for 10 minutes or so before spooning or piping the cake batter into buttered muffin moulds. Make sure that you fill all 12 moulds or otherwise the financiers will be too deep and will not cook in the given time. Heat your oven to 195°C/175°C fan/385°F/gas mark 5–6 while you are waiting for the batter to rest.
5. Place the muffin tin in the centre of the oven and bake for 8 minutes before removing. The financiers will seem a little soft, but that is the idea. Let them cool in the tin for at least 10 minutes before removing and consuming with large dollops of coffee cream.

For friends

For the weekend

Weekends are a relatively recent addition to our lives. Throughout our working life before Honey & Co, we had our days off during the week and spent the end of it cooking for those who were off work. When we opened Honey & Co, it was just the two of us and we decided, out of necessity, not to open on Sundays, thinking we might revisit this someday. Those first Sundays off were not spent sleeping or relaxing, but at work, prepping and cleaning. As the team grew and we were no longer doing everything ourselves, Sundays evolved and we started to use this day to catch up on much-needed sleep. Suddenly the week had a different rhythm to it; for the first time in our lives we got to say goodbye at the end of the week, close the shop and truly (almost) clock off – at least from the day-to-day duties of restaurant life. We could now give the team, the machines and ourselves a good rest, and we would all meet again on Monday, rested and restored, happy to see each other and talk about our weekend. This may sound normal to most people, but for us it was a complete novelty, a delightful ritual which we relished.

Five years on, we still close on Sundays, and while we truly love our working week, we are no longer looking to revisit the idea of opening up. We discovered weekends. We are weekend people now and we do weekend things so we have something to talk about on Monday. One time, we went to Paris to meet friends; croissant for breakfast, an afternoon of beers and ice cream in the Place des Vosges, a bistro dinner, way too much food, way too much wine… we had to sleep it off on the train back.

Another memorable one was the country house party we went to. About to miss the train, we ran around the UK's busiest railway station trying to find the right platform. I was balancing a rapidly-melting chocolate mousse cake against my shirt front, while my wife's situation was much worse – her wrap dress was unwrapping, giving our fellow travellers much more than a glimpse. We didn't make that train and were stupidly late for the party, but we certainly remember that weekend, and I'm sure whoever saw the tubby chocolate-covered man and the half-naked woman running around Clapham Junction that day will not quickly forget it either.

We are now weekend pros. We have learned that the truly great weekends are the ones we don't remember; the ones when we sleep in and wake up lazy. Eating breakfast and reading the papers, discussing important nothings like the spare bedroom furniture or the latest sex scandal at work (there's always a sex scandal at work); catching up on the phone with family and friends; a leisurely trip to the butchers' or to the farmers' market; Netflix and chill; an afternoon nap; and then some time spent in the kitchen, cooking purely for the pleasure of cooking – taking on bread-making, a pickling or preserving project, or trying out a recipe we've been wanting to cook for a while. Cooking for friends who are coming over, or just for us. Going to bed early, gently putting the last week away and preparing for a new one. Starting work on Monday with nothing to tell. Just a weekend, as it should be.

Fig and feta pide

Autumn is when we like to go away. The hectic holiday season is over; beaches and restaurants all around the Med are empty of us sun-crazed Northerners; the sun, who has mostly exhausted her heat in the summer, is now kinder, more gentle. This is when everyone without kids in school goes away, so we board a plane to a Mediterranean shore with the very young, the retired and the gay. And so it is that our holidays are always flavoured with figs – late season, still warm from the summer sun.

We have strong memories of a tree on a rural road on a Greek island. It was laden with the most amazingly sweet figs, as many as you could stomach. We would drive there especially.

We remember tearing ourselves from work after an exhausting summer to head to the Balearic Islands. We were greeted in a hotel carpark by a huge fig tree. We parked our little rental car in its shade and took our first bite of the summer – it was then and there that our holiday started.

We all have our little milestones in the year, those recurring events that make us pause and think, 'This time last year…' or 'This time next year…'. The Proms, the first magnolia tree blooming, fireworks on Guy Fawkes' night. For us it's always autumn, and it is always flavoured with figs. It is when the Jewish year starts; it is when the Day of Atonement falls; it is when we got married. All those sweet and serious life moments are connected by the honeyed sweetness, the resiny undertone, the giving flesh and the crunch of seeds in a fig.

Makes 6

For the dough

300g/10½oz/2¼ cups flour

1 tsp sugar

1 tsp salt

½ tsp freshly ground black pepper

1 tbsp nigella seeds

a pinch of cayenne pepper

15g/½oz fresh yeast or 1 sachet
(7g/¼oz) dried active yeast

1 tsp honey

150g/5¼oz/⅔ cup yogurt

For the filling

100g/3½oz feta

50g/1¾oz/¼ cup yogurt

½ tsp dried oregano

½ tsp sumac (you could substitute
with zest of 1 lemon)

For the toppings

1 green chilli

3 tbsp olive oil

6–8 figs (depending on size)

1 small bag of washed
baby spinach

salt and freshly ground
black pepper

a few sprigs of fresh thyme or a
pinch of dried oregano

1. Place the flour, sugar, salt, black pepper, nigella seeds and cayenne pepper in a large mixing bowl. Dissolve the yeast in 100ml/3½fl oz/ scant ½ cup of water and stir in the honey, then add this, along with the yogurt, to the dry ingredients. Knead together to form a nice, supple dough (you can use a mixer with a dough hook if you wish, but it is really easy to mix by hand). Cover the bowl with a cloth or cling film, set in a warm place and allow the dough to double in size. It will take about 1 hour in a warm room, slightly longer if it's cold.
2. Make the filling by crumbling the feta into a small bowl and mixing with the yogurt, oregano and sumac to create a paste.
3. For the topping, slice the green chilli into rounds, place in a small dish and cover with the olive oil. Cut the figs into 4–5 slices.
4. Once the dough has proved, divide it into 6 evenly sized lumps. Roughly stretch each piece into an oval boat-shape measuring around 20cm/8 inches long and 8cm/3¼ inches wide. Put a tablespoon of the feta filling on each, spreading it over the centre. Add a handful of baby spinach, then slices of fig. Top with the chilli slices and the oil, using it all up. Season with salt and pepper, and sprinkle with some leaves from the sprigs of thyme or dried oregano.
5. Pinch the sides of the dough up around the edges, then pinch each end of the oval into a point to create a pide boat. Leave to prove again and, while you are waiting, heat your oven to 220°C/200°C fan/425°F/ gas mark 7. By the time the oven is up to temperature, the boats will be ready to pop in. Bake for 10–12 minutes until beautifully golden. Serve warm.

Turkish yogurt bread with aubergine filling

Not that long ago, if you wanted to get good bread, you had to make an effort to find it, or indeed bake it yourself. In the last few years, though, there seems to be an artisan bakery under every railway arch, offering fresh loaves to those of us who feel that their Marmite and cheese deserve a better bed. We all profess to avoid carbs and banish gluten from our lives, but evidence to the contrary is all around: good bread is back (a breanaissance, if you will).

There is no reason to bake bread at home unless you really enjoy it, and (as those of us who regularly do so, know already) there are plenty of joys to be had in the process. Like that magical moment when flour and water suddenly become something else – a shiny, elastic dough. Or when the dough starts to rise, invisible forces within it bubbling gently. The smell of the dough before it bakes, as it is baking, once it is out of the oven. That special warmth that a fresh loaf radiates as you hold it in your hands – like holding a sleeping puppy.

Aside from the sensual delights, there is great satisfaction that comes with taking part in a process as old as human civilization, and almost as widespread. Not forgetting the immense sense of pride in the beautiful thing you have just made.

Bread is usually an accompaniment – we fill it, top it, dip it, mop our plates with it, toss it on salads and soups. In this Turkish-inspired recipe, the bread takes centre stage: the dough is made with a mixture of flours for a complex flavour, and is enriched with olive oil, egg and plenty of yogurt, which gives it a smooth milky texture and a wonderful tang. Aubergines, herbs and cheese are added to the dough, and the whole thing is wrapped around more aubergines and tied in a jaunty topknot for cuteness.

This is good picnic fare and will serve you well when lots of people come around. Or just bake it and leave it on the kitchen counter for the household to nibble on as they walk past. It won't last long, even in very small households.

Turkish yogurt bread with aubergine filling

To make 1 large free-form loaf

For the aubergine filling

2 small aubergines (about 300g/10½oz each)

4 tbsp olive oil

1 tsp salt

1 tbsp sherry vinegar

2 tbsp dried or fresh oregano

1 tsp chopped rosemary

1 garlic clove, peeled and crushed

1 small bunch of parsley, chopped

For the dough

30g/1oz fresh yeast or 15g/½oz dried active yeast

2 tsp sugar

200g/7oz/2 cups spelt flour

500g/1lb 2oz/3½ cups strong bread flour

2 tsp salt

200g/7oz/scant 1 cup yogurt

1 egg

30ml/2 tbsp olive oil

half the aubergine filing (the half without the parsley)

100g/3½oz/1⅓ cups grated Parmesan or pecorino

To finish the loaf

half the aubergine filling (the half with the chopped parsley)

2 long sprigs of rosemary

a drizzle of olive oil

a sprinkling of sea salt

1. Heat the oven to 220°C/200°C fan/425°F/gas mark 7. Line a large tray with baking paper. Cut the aubergines in large dice and place on the tray. Drizzle with the oil and sprinkle with the salt.

2. Bake for 10 minutes, then remove from the oven and stir around a little. Return to the oven for another 10 minutes until the aubergines are golden. Remove to a large bowl and, while they are still hot, add the vinegar, oregano, rosemary and garlic, and mix well. Put half the mixture in a separate bowl and stir the fresh, chopped parsley into that half.

3. Put the yeast and sugar in a bowl with 250ml/8¾fl oz/generous 1 cup warm water and stir to dissolve. Put the flours and salt in the bowl of an electric mixer with a dough hook, add the yogurt, egg and olive oil, and start mixing on a slow speed. Gradually add the yeasted water until well-combined. Then add the parsley-free portion of the aubergines and the grated cheese, and work to a smooth dough (you may need a little more warm water to form a lovely, loose dough). Transfer to a large, oiled bowl and cover. Set aside to prove until doubled in size. This will take about 1½ hours in a warm kitchen.

4. Remove the dough to a lightly-floured surface and press down to form a large disc. Pop the other half of the filling in the middle and lift the sides of the dough up around it to form a rough 'money bag'. Scrunch the top together to seal, lift onto the lined baking tray and wrap the sprigs of rosemary around the topknot. Set aside in a warm place to prove until doubled in size for the second time (about 1 hour).

5. Heat your oven to 220°C/200°C fan/425°F/gas mark 7. Bake the bread for 15 minutes, then reduce the heat to 200°C/180°C fan/400°F/gas mark 6 and bake for a further 20 minutes. By now, the bread should have a nice golden colour and should lift easily from the tray. If it doesn't, bake for a further 5–10 minutes. Remove from the oven, drizzle with a little olive oil and sprinkle with sea salt. Place on a wire rack so that the bread doesn't steam on the baking tray, and serve as soon as you are ready.

Jerusalem sesame bread

This recipe came to me from Yonit Naftali, an editor at Israel's top food magazine. We went to high school together in Jerusalem, a stone's throw from the old city walls. I had a huge crush on her. She had a boyfriend all through high school but enjoyed the attention all the same. We became friends, and then we became good friends. On breaks and after school we would go to the Jaffa gate of the Old City, where vendors sold these sesame breads from wooden handcarts. With your bread you always got a little za'atar wrapped in old newspaper. We would sit on the stone steps outside the Old City, dipping chunks of bread – the crunchy sesame crust revealing the soft, pillowy inside – in the herby, tangy za'atar powder, and we would talk for hours about whatever it is awkward teenagers talk about; in our case, it was mostly about food and cooking.

Years passed, and we turned from good friends to very good friends. At one point the tables flipped and she had a crush on me, but I had already met the love of my life. She (the love) in turn introduced her (Yonit) to one of her good friends. It was a set-up at one of our earliest joint parties. Yonit and the friend locked lips on that first night and they haven't parted since. They got married on one of the hottest days of one of the hottest Augusts on record, in a tent in the desert – the wedding cake my wife baked for them collapsed in the heat. They now have two kids: a boy and a girl; both adorable, yet neither is named after either of us.

I recently crashed in their Tel Aviv flat late one night, hungry. Yonit pulled these out of the freezer for us. We were tearing bits of bread that tasted just like the real thing (actually better), dipping them in yogurt, with some radishes and olives as well. For hours we talked. About this recipe, other recipes and many things; whatever it is adults talk about.

This is a great pre-dinner treat served with some dips, or indeed with za'atar. It is great for sandwiches. And it freezes very well – great to pull out when old friends drop by.

Jerusalem sesame bread

To make 8 bread sticks or
1 large loaf (see opposite)

For the dough

500g/1lb 2oz/3½ cups
strong flour

70g/2½oz/generous ⅓ cup sugar

20g/¾oz fresh yeast or
1 heaped tsp dried active yeast

260–280ml/8¾–9½fl oz/scant 1¼
cups warm water

1 egg yolk

1½ tsp salt

2 tbsp olive oil

For the topping

100–120g/3½–4¼oz/¾ cup
sesame seeds, or any other mix of
seeds you fancy

1 tsp sea salt

100ml/3½fl oz/scant ½ cup
olive oil (yes, that much!)

1. Put the flour in a mixer bowl with a dough hook attachment. Dissolve the sugar and yeast in 200ml/7fl oz/scant 1 cup of the warm water and gradually add it to the flour while mixing. Add as much of the remaining water as is needed to help form a smooth ball of dough.

2. Knead the dough for about 2–3 minutes to develop the gluten and then add the egg yolk, salt and olive oil in a slow, steady stream while the machine is still turning. The dough will collapse, and incorporating these ingredients will seem impossible, but continue kneading until it all comes together again (about 2–3 minutes).

3. Remove the bowl from the machine and cover with a cloth or cling film. Leave the dough to prove in a warm place until doubled in size (it will take about 1–1½ hours).

4. Put two large baking trays nearby. Put some cold water in a small bowl, and tip the sesame seeds onto a flat tray. Moisten your hands with the water and transfer the dough from the bowl to your workbench. Flatten it a little. It will be a very wet, soft dough but try not to add any flour at all. Split the dough into 8 evenly-sized lumps.

5. Dip your palms in the water again, then grab a portion of dough and squeeze it into a rough log. Make sure it is quite wet, then dip the log in the sesame seeds. Flip to dip the other side, then lift carefully and place on one of the baking trays. Repeat with all the dough. Leave a little space between each bread stick to allow for expansion while proving (I usually fit four on a tray). Leave uncovered to double in size (this will take 30–60 minutes).

6. Heat your oven to 240°C/220°C fan/475°F/gas mark 9. Mix the olive oil with the sea salt in a cup.

7. Once the dough sticks are fully proved, bake in the centre of the oven for 8 minutes, then rotate the tray and bake for another 2–3 minutes or until golden all over. As soon as they come out of the oven, brush generously with the salted olive oil. Leave on the tray for 3–4 minutes, then lift off to a cooling rack.

8. These are best eaten warm and fresh with something like radish tzatziki on the side. Add a little dish of za'atar, and have alternate bites – one with za'atar, one with tzatziki.

9. As mentioned above, these freeze really well once baked – simply allow to thaw, then heat in the oven at 200°C/180°C fan/400°F/gas mark 6 for 5 minutes (don't microwave them, as they will become chewy). They also work superbly to make the best sandwiches in town (see ideas for fillings on pages 142–3).

For a large tray-baked sandwich loaf

Usually we make the dough opposite into eight bread sticks, but sometimes, when we are in a rush or want to make a quick bread that can be sliced into plenty of easy-to-transport sandwiches, we make this large loaf.

1. After the first proving (step 3 opposite), simply oil a deep oven tray, sprinkle it with sesame seeds, put the dough on top, then push with moist hands all the way to the corners of the tray. Sprinkle with more seeds. Prove and bake it as you would the bread sticks, the only difference being the baking time.
2. Start at 240°C/220°C fan/475°F/gas mark 9 for 10 minutes, then reduce the oven temperature to 200°C/180°C fan/400°F/gas mark 6 and bake for a further 10 minutes. Open the oven, rotate the tray and bake for a final 5 minutes. Remove and brush with the salted oil (you will only need half the quantity listed opposite).
3. Cool the bread completely in the tray it was baked in, then use a sharp knife to loosen the edges – it should simply drop out. Slice the cooled bread in half horizontally, as you would when cutting a cake in layers. Fill with anything and/or everything, pop the top layer back on to cover, and slice to the required size.
4. This bread freezes really well too, so it is worth making a batch for the freezer.

Harissa and lemon chicken sandwich

Makes 6–8 sandwiches, depending on the size

150g/5¼oz/⅔ cup plain natural Greek-style yogurt

2 tbsp rose harissa paste

1 tsp sweet paprika

6 chicken thighs, skinless and boneless

2 preserved lemons (skin only, discard the pulp), finely chopped

1 small bunch of coriander, leaves picked and roughly chopped (about 20g/¾oz), plus more to serve

juice of ½ lemon

Jerusalem sesame bread (see page 138)

Little Gem lettuce leaves (optional)

salt and freshly ground black pepper, to taste

1. Mix the yogurt with the harissa paste and paprika. Remove three tablespoons to a bowl and set it aside in the fridge for later. Add the raw chicken thighs to the remaining yogurt mixture, season with salt and pepper, and mix well to coat. You can cook them straight away or, even better, leave them to marinate in the fridge for a couple of hours, if you have the time. They will hold well for at least 24 hours.

2. Heat the oven to 220°C/200°C fan/425°F/gas mark 7. Place a wire rack on a baking tray and pop the chicken thighs on the rack, flat-side facing up. Roast in the oven for 15 minutes, then remove and cool.

3. Slice the cooked chicken thinly and combine with the yogurt-harissa mixture that you set aside. Add the preserved lemon, chopped coriander and lemon juice, mix well and adjust the seasoning if needed. Use to fill your sandwiches.

4. A good accompaniment to this filling is Little Gem lettuce, either shredded outer leaves or whole inner leaves from the heart, and some more freshly picked coriander leaves.

Roasted tomato and manouri cheese sandwich

Makes 6–8 sandwiches, depending on the size

4 large plum tomatoes, cut into slices about 2cm/¾ inch thick

2 tbsp olive oil

a sprinkling of sugar

a sprinkling of dried oregano

a sprinkling of whole coriander seeds

2 thick slices of manouri (about 240g/8½oz)

1 garlic clove, halved

Jerusalem sesame bread (see page 138)

leaves from a few sprigs of mint

salt and freshly ground black pepper, to taste

1. Heat the oven to 220°C/200°C fan/425°F/gas mark 7. Place the slices of tomato on a roasting tray and drizzle with the olive oil. Season with salt and pepper, sprinkle on the sugar and dried oregano, then drop a few coriander seeds on each tomato slice. Roast in the oven for 10 minutes. Add the two slices of manouri, flip them in the oily juices that have formed on the tray, and return the tray to the oven to roast for a further 5 minutes.

2. Rub the halved garlic all over the surface of your bread. Put a few tomato pieces on each slice, crumble the manouri into small chunks, and add to the tomato. Season with salt and pepper and top with the picked mint leaves.

Tuna, capers and roasted pepper sandwich

Makes 6–8 sandwiches, depending on the size

2 tins tuna in oil (about 320g/11¼oz), drained

2 tbsp capers

2 preserved lemons (skin only, discard the pulp), finely chopped

2 tbsp rose harissa paste

1 small bunch of parsley, leaves picked and chopped

2 tbsp olive oil

2 roasted peppers (roast in a hot oven for 10 minutes)

4 hard-boiled eggs

Jerusalem sesame bread (see page 138)

1. Put the drained tuna in a large mixing bowl. Add the capers, preserved lemon, rose harissa, parsley and olive oil, and mix well. Use to fill the sandwiches.

2. Peel the roasted peppers, tear them into thin strips and lay them on top of the tuna. Finally, peel and slice the hard-boiled eggs and add to the sandwiches, allowing about half an egg per sandwich.

M'sabaha

In Middle Eastern cooking the chickpea is king. 'Hummus' in Arabic simply means chickpea. The dip that is sold at deli counters across the world (and in the US, you can even get it in squeezy bottles, like ketchup) started life as a hearty workman's breakfast. The chickpeas would cook overnight to soft obedience before being mashed up and whipped into a creamy purée with a bit of tahini and minimal seasoning, then ladled hot into bowls to be eaten like porridge. This cheap and tasty treat would give sustenance through the day's hard work under the blazing hot sun. To this day traditional hummus vendors close their shop before noon.

Our friend Erez starts his working day at a stall behind Tel Aviv's Carmel market with a bowl of hot hummus. He doesn't plough fields or herd cattle – he writes scripts for a living and teaches in the air-conditioned halls of the University, but his days are long and busy, and this breakfast keeps him going.

M'sabaha is the at-home version. It uses the same ingredients, but instead of mashing them together, they are kept as themselves to create a stew: the chickpeas keep their pleasant texture, the tahini thickens the cooking liquid, and the tatbila on top gives it all a lovely lift. Even though pulses for breakfast are not uncommon in this country, we suspect most of you would opt to have this version of baked beans at other times of day – as the main meal with some bread, or in a smaller portion as a starter. Any leftovers can be mashed up to make a hummus dip.

M'sabaha

Makes 4 generous portions

For the chickpeas

125g/4½oz/¾ cup chickpeas, soaked overnight (or for a minimum of 8 hours) in plenty of cold water

½ tsp bicarbonate of soda

1 tomato, cut into quarters

2 sprigs of rosemary

2 sprigs of sage

6 garlic cloves, peeled

1 tsp cumin seeds

1 tsp salt

1 tsp ground cumin

50ml/1¾fl oz/3½ tbsp olive oil

For the tatbila and other toppings

2 long green chillies (the Turkish ones are the best)

flesh and juice from 1 peeled lemon

2 garlic cloves, peeled

a pinch of salt

1 tbsp olive oil

2 tbsp raw tahini paste

a pinch of smoked paprika and chopped parsley (optional)

1. Lift the soaked chickpeas out of their water with a slotted spoon and place them in a saucepan. Cover with fresh water and bring to the boil. Skim away any scum that comes to the top and add the bicarbonate of soda. It should bubble up again with lots of foam. Reduce the heat and use a spoon to remove the foam. Keep the water at a rolling boil for 8 minutes.

2. Drain the chickpeas, then pour in just enough fresh hot water to cover them again and add the tomato, rosemary, sage, garlic and cumin seeds. Set back on the heat on the lowest setting, cover and simmer until the chickpeas are fully softened. This can take up to 40–50 minutes, depending on the freshness of the chickpeas, but test them after 30 minutes. Once they are soft (but not falling apart), add the salt, ground cumin and olive oil, half-cover with the lid and simmer for a final 10 minutes.

3. While the chickpeas finish cooking, quickly blitz the chillies, lemon flesh and garlic to a paste in a food processor. Tip into a small bowl, add the pinch of salt and the olive oil and stir well.

4. Remove and discard the stems of the herbs and the tomato skins from the chickpea pan. Taste and adjust the seasoning, if necessary.

5. To serve, spoon the chickpeas into bowls, drizzle each with some raw tahini and top with as much tatbila as you like. A sprinkling of smoked paprika and parsley is also nice, but not essential.

Shishbarak

These dumplings from Palestinian cuisine are so labour-intensive that they usually take a whole family, or at least a few people, to make. The dough is rolled paper-thin, the filling is prepared, teeny-tiny dumplings are filled, sealed and cooked for hours in a sauce made with kashk (fermented, dried yogurt), everyone taking turns stirring the pot, which cannot be left alone for a minute, as otherwise the dumplings will catch. The result is unlike anything else: the sauce silky, the dumplings yielding their rich filling as they melt in the mouth… Delicious though this is, we could not in good conscience ask anyone to prepare them the traditional way, so we took some liberties, borrowing some Italian techniques and offering a few shortcuts. This is still a demanding preparation but is certainly manageable for one (determined) person, and definitely worth the effort. You will need to start this a day in advance for best results, so that the salt rub can penetrate the meat to give it a great flavour.

Shishbarak

To make 30 dumplings, enough for 4–6 portions

To salt and cook the ribs

1 tsp each of ground ginger, cumin, cinnamon and pimento/allspice

2 tbsp Maldon sea salt

850g/1kg/1lb 14oz–2lb 4oz short ribs or Jacob's ladder

For the yogurt sauce

500ml/18fl oz/2 cups beef cooking liquid, strained

300g/10½oz/1⅓ cups yogurt

1 tbsp cornflour

1 egg yolk

For the filling

2 tbsp olive oil

2 large onions, peeled and very finely chopped (about 240g/8½oz)

all the meat from the ribs (about 350g/12⅓oz), chopped

100g/3½oz/¾ cup dried currants, soaked in some water

100ml/3½fl oz/scant ½ cup yogurt sauce (above)

1 tsp ground cumin

½ tsp chilli flakes, plus an additional pinch to serve

1 tsp ground cinnamon

1 small bunch of parsley, chopped

salt and freshly ground black pepper

For the dough

2 eggs

400g/14oz/scant 3 cups '00' flour or strong bread flour, plus more for dusting

1 tsp salt

80g/2¾oz soft butter

1. Mix the ground spices with the salt and season the meat generously all over. Wrap in cling film and place in the fridge overnight, or for at least 6 hours.

2. Heat your oven to 220°C/200°C fan/425°F/gas mark 7. Roast the meat uncovered in a roasting tin for 20 minutes. Reduce the oven to 200°C/180°C fan/400°F/gas mark 6, cover the meat with water and return to the oven for 1 hour.

3. Carefully open the oven (it will be steamy), baste the meat and gently turn it in the liquid. Reduce the heat to 180°C/160°C fan/350°F/gas mark 4 and cook for another hour. Now check whether the meat is very soft and falling off the bone. If it is a particularly tough piece, it may require another 30 minutes or so. Once it feels soft, remove from the oven and allow to cool a little in the liquid. When it is cold enough to handle, strain the cooking liquid into a bowl (to use in the sauce). Shred the meat into another bowl, discarding any bones and sinew.

4. To make the sauce, boil the beef cooking liquid in a saucepan and reduce by half to intensify the flavour – you want to end up with 250ml/8¾fl oz/generous 1 cup of concentrated stock. Mix the yogurt with the cornflour and egg yolk, then slowly whisk into the beef stock until well combined. Set aside until you are ready to use.

5. Heat the oil for the filling in a large pan and cook the onions slowly on a medium-low heat until they are very soft and starting to caramelise to a golden-brown colour – it will take 15–20 minutes. Add the meat to the onions and mix really well, then remove from the heat and stir in all the remaining filling ingredients (keep 2 tablespoons each of the currants and parsley to one side). Once cooled, roll the filling into 30 evenly sized balls (about 20–30g/¾–1oz each) and set in the fridge.

6. Place the eggs, flour, salt and butter for the dough in a food processor, and blitz to a crumb-like consistency. Add just enough water to bring together to a ball (100–120ml/3½–4¼fl oz/½ cup). Remove and wrap in cling film before setting in the fridge to rest for at least an hour.

7. Lightly flour your work surface and roll the dough as thinly as you can (or use a pasta machine, if you have one). Place balls of the meat filling in a line about 2cm/¾ inch up from the bottom part of the dough (closest to you), roughly 4cm/1½ inches apart. Brush the edges lightly with a little water. Fold the dough over to create little ravioli-like parcels and press the dough all around each ball to seal. Cut into rectangles. Grab two diagonal corners and pinch them together to create a tortellini-like shape. Repeat until all your pasta is filled. Store in the fridge (or even the freezer) till you are ready to cook.

8. Boil plenty of salted water and blanch the dumplings for about 3–4 minutes (6–8 if you are cooking from frozen). While they are blanching, heat the yogurt sauce in a large frying pan over a low heat. When the dumplings are cooked, pop them in the frying pan and swirl gently to coat with the sauce. Transfer to a serving plate, sprinkle with the remaining currants, chopped parsley and chilli flakes. Serve immediately.

For the weekend

Celeriac mafrum

We are never really interested in innovative food. The food we like most – to cook and eat – is traditional and homey; the more specific to a particular area and culture, the better. That said, some of these dishes simply do not stand the test of time, and must be tinkered with a bit in order for us to enjoy them still. Like mafrum: a North African dish of gently-spiced meat stuffed in a root vegetable or artichokes and cooked slowly in a lemony sauce. The result is nothing short of sublime – the lemony broth marries with the savoury meat and the sweet celeriac – magic, but the preparation is too time-consuming and, frankly, painful, even for a pair of slightly masochistic professional chefs like us. The prospect of hollowing out a celeriac for stuffing is too much, and I don't think many people would or should try it at home.

It would be such a shame to let this beautiful preparation become extinct, so instead of hollowing out the celeriac, we use slices of it to sandwich the filling, and cook it like that. You end up with a burger of sorts that carries all the flavour of centuries of tradition. If you do give this dish a go (please give this dish a go), pat yourself on the back for your role in its preservation.

To make 4 celeriac 'sandwiches', 1
per person as part of a larger meal

For the meat filling

600g/1lb 5oz/2½ cups
minced beef

½ leek, washed and finely chopped
(about 120g/4¼oz)

zest of ½ lemon

1 garlic clove, peeled
and minced

1 small bunch of parsley, chopped
(keep the stalks)

1 tbsp ground cumin

1 tbsp ground coriander

1 tsp salt

a pinch of freshly ground
black pepper

1 tsp ground turmeric

1 tsp bicarbonate of soda

For the celeriac 'sandwiches'

2 celeriac, peeled

25g/1oz soft butter

For the stock

2 tbsp olive oil

the celeriac trimmings
(see method, step 2)

½ leek, sliced and washed

3 slices of lemon

4 garlic cloves, peeled and halved

1 tbsp coriander seeds

parsley stalks (see above)

To finish

juice of ½ lemon

1. Mix all the ingredients for the filling together and divide into four equal amounts.
2. Trim the celeriacs into rough spheres, then slice each one into four even slices, each about 2 cm/¾ inch thick. Keep all the trimmings, tops and bottoms for the stock, but discard the peel.
3. Place a quarter of the filling onto a slice of celeriac and top with another slice to make a 'sandwich', pressing it down to flatten the meat so it reaches the sides. Butter the outsides of the celeriac 'sandwich' and season with salt and pepper. Repeat with the rest of the celeriac and filling, and place the 'sandwiches' in a deep roasting tray (or a large casserole) that can fit four slices of the celeriac comfortably in one layer.
4. Heat your oven to 220°C/200°C fan/425°F/gas mark 7. Make the stock by heating the oil and sweating the celeriac trimmings, leek, lemon slices, garlic and coriander seeds until the vegetables soften (about 10–15 minutes). Add 1 litre/1¾ pints/4⅓ cups of water and the parsley stalks and cook for 15 minutes on a steady simmer before straining. You should end up with 500–600ml/18–21fl oz/2–2½ cups of stock.
5. While the stock is simmering and reducing down, roast the celeriac sandwiches in the centre of the oven for 10 minutes, then use a spatula to gently flip them over before roasting for another 10 minutes.
6. Carefully pour the hot stock into the roasting tray, cover and return to the oven for 15 minutes. Remove and baste the celeriac sandwiches all over, re-cover and return to the oven for a further 15 minutes. Remove again and baste well, add the lemon juice and return to the oven, uncovered this time, to roast for the final 15 minutes before serving.

Honey and spice cookies

These are the ones we make for Valentine's Day. Loosely based on German Pfeffernüsse, they are somewhere between a cake and a biscuit, their texture unlike any other baked goods: moist and slightly crumbly. They deliver on flavour with a lovely mix of spice and sweetness. The pink icing not only gives them that Valentine's look but also provides the most dainty and delicate crust. Whenever we make them, they always get the love.

Makes 22–24

For the cookies

120ml/4¼fl oz/½ cup strong coffee

50ml/1¾fl oz/3½ tbsp vegetable oil

50g/1¾oz butter

140g/5oz/scant ¾ cup dark brown sugar

180g/6¼oz/⅔ cup honey

1 tsp ground ginger

2 tsp ground cinnamon

½ tsp ground nutmeg

zest of 1 clementine or orange

420g/14¾oz/scant 3¼ cups plain flour

½ tsp bicarbonate of soda

1 tsp baking powder

1 tsp vinegar

For the icing

200g/7oz/scant 1½ cups icing sugar

1 tbsp pink juice, squeezed from raspberries, strawberries or redcurrants

2 tbsp milk

1. Put the coffee, oil, butter, sugar and honey in a saucepan. Mix all the other ingredients apart from the vinegar together in a large bowl.
2. Heat the honey-oil mixture until the butter has melted and it just starts to boil. Remove from the heat, stir in the vinegar and then pour into the dry ingredients. Use a large spoon to mix really well until the dough is smooth and thick. Cover the bowl with cling film and place in the fridge for about an hour.
3. Heat your oven to 200°C/180°C fan/400°F/gas mark 6 and line two large trays with baking paper.
4. Dampen your palms with a little cold water and shape the dough into 22–24 balls (each about 35g/1¼oz, give or take). Re-moisten your palms between each cookie. Set them on the trays with a little space (about 2cm/¾ inch) between them, as they will spread when baked. Bake for 15–16 minutes until they dome up. They will still feel very soft, but will set as they cool on the tray.
5. Mix the icing sugar, juice and milk together to form a thin, pinkish icing. Place the cookies on a rack and use a teaspoon or a piping bag to cover the top of each with icing, allowing it drip down the dome. Leave on the rack to set entirely before removing from the rack and serving.

For the weekend

Medjool date, honey and macadamia breakfast loaf

The unique flavour of rich, artisan honey comes through beautifully here and is really worthy of the expense. Together with the Christmassy spicing, it makes a perfect foil for chunks of toffee-sweet medjool dates and buttery macadamia nuts.

This is a really large loaf, and you will need to use a big tin. If you are not sure about the size of your tin, just make sure you only fill it three-quarters full. This recipe bakes nicely in two smaller tins too, but please read my note about adjusting baking times at the end.

Makes 1 large 2-kg/4lb 8-oz loaf
or 2 smaller ones

For the cake

150ml/5¼fl oz/scant ⅔ cup
full-fat milk

110g/4oz/⅓ cup honey – use
a high-quality, raw honey for
best results

50g/1¾oz salted butter

280g/10oz/2 heaped cups
self-raising flour

200g/7oz/1 cup sugar

zest of 1 orange

skin of 1 clementine,
finely chopped

1 tsp ground cinnamon

1 tsp ground nutmeg

200g/7oz/scant 1¼ cups medjool
dates, pitted and roughly cut

130g/4½oz/1 cup
macadamia nuts

2 eggs

For the topping

50g/1¾oz/⅓ cup
macadamia nuts

2 tbsp demerara sugar

1. Heat your oven to 180°C/160°C fan/350°F/gas mark 4. Line your loaf tin(s) with a sheet of baking paper.
2. Place the milk, honey and butter in a small pan and heat gently until the butter has melted. In the meantime, mix the rest of the ingredients apart from the eggs in a large bowl. Pour in the melted butter mixture and use a large spoon to stir until just combined. Add the eggs and stir again until fully combined.
3. Transfer to the baking tin, top with the macadamia nuts and sprinkle with the demerara sugar. Bake in the centre of the oven for 30 minutes. Open the oven and rotate the cake for an even bake, then leave for a further 20–25 minutes. It should feel lovely and bouncy when you press it. If you are using two smaller tins, they will bake in a shorter time – I would rotate them after 20 minutes and then leave for another 20 minutes to bake fully.

Rich fruit cakes

What do you call a Brazil nut in Brazil? A Spanish omelette in Spain is just an omelette. No one in Jaffa has ever heard of a Jaffa cake; but if you ask for an English cake there, or anywhere in Israel, everyone will know what you mean. A simple sponge, baked in a loaf tin, with some dried fruit inside, usually glacé cherries in fluorescent red and green, and some candied orange peel. In fact, we call all loaf cakes English cake, or sometimes English, for short.

We've been living in this country for twelve years now, and we have had many cakes traditional to it, none of them bearing any resemblance to what we grew up thinking was the national English cake. We often wonder how this cake came to get its name – maybe a fruit cake washed up on the Jaffa shore and was discovered by an intrepid baker; perhaps a seedless seed cake or a Madeira that someone had embellished with some glacé cherries?

As preparations travel from country to country, they adapt to their new culture and home, the local needs and local produce. Sometime they change so much that all that is left is a name, without even a memory of the original. Someone should do some research into it, but not us. We do our research into the recipes themselves, not their history or nomenclature, and we often find ourselves in need of a good cake – one you can mix, bake and keep for a bit. Something uncomplicated but fun to eat, good to have around the house when the afternoon comes, served alongside a strong coffee when something sweet is required, or when friends drop by unannounced (although we live in London – no one ever drops by unannounced; that only happens in the countryside or in cookery columns). We came up with these two. One has a light eastern spicing, pistachios for texture and dried cranberries (a nod to those glacé cherries that we don't ever use). The other uses a load of dried currants and raisins, mixed with some bitter marmalade, and carries a distinct note of British baking, inspired by Delia. It doesn't get more English than that.

Don't get too hung up on specific ingredients here. You can change the fruit, nuts and spices to whatever you have in the house or whatever you prefer, and as long as you stick to the same quantities and use a little common sense, you'll end up with a good 'English' cake.

Marmalade and dried fruit cake

Makes a large 1-kg/2lb 4-oz loaf

100g/3½oz/¾ cup wholemeal flour

100g/3½oz/¾ cup plain flour

1 tsp baking powder

1 tsp ground cinnamon

1 tsp ground nutmeg

1 tsp ground ginger

a pinch of salt

250g/9oz/scant 2 cups mixed dried currants, cranberries and raisins

zest of 1 lemon

zest of 1 orange

150g/5¼oz butter, plus more for greasing

200g/7oz/1 cup + 2 tbsp golden caster sugar

2 eggs

100g/3½oz/⅓ cup orange marmalade

1 tbsp demerara sugar, for topping

1. Heat your oven to 180°C/160°C fan/350°F/gas mark 4 and butter and line your loaf tin with baking paper.
2. Mix the flours, baking powder, spices and salt with the dried fruit and set aside.
3. Use a large spoon or a mixer with a paddle attachment to cream the lemon and orange zest with the butter and caster sugar until very fluffy, then add the eggs one at a time and mix to combine. Add the flour-fruit mixture and, once that is incorporated, spoon in the marmalade and combine to an even batter.
4. Transfer to the lined baking tin, smooth the top and sprinkle with the demerara sugar. Bake in the centre of the oven for 30 minutes, turn the tin, then bake for another 25–30 minutes until the cake feels bouncy to the touch. Allow to cool in the tin before removing. You can store this cake at room temperature for about 3–4 days.

Pistachio and cranberry cake

Makes a large 1-kg/2lb 4-oz loaf

200g/7oz/1½ cups
self-raising flour

1 tsp ground fennel seeds

5 cardamom pods, ground to a
powder (pods and seeds)

1 tsp vanilla essence, or seeds
from ½ vanilla pod

a pinch of salt

150g/5¼oz/1 cup
dried cranberries

100g/3½oz/¾ cup whole
shelled pistachios

zest of 2 limes

150g/5¼oz butter, plus more
for greasing

150g/5¼oz/generous ¾ cup
golden caster sugar

2 eggs

100g/3½oz/⅓ cup cherry,
raspberry or redcurrant jam

juice of 1 lime

1 tbsp demerara sugar, for topping

1. Heat your oven to 180°C/160°C fan/350°F/gas mark 4 and butter and line your loaf tin with baking paper.
2. Mix the flour, spices, salt, cranberries and pistachios, then set aside.
3. Use a large spoon or a mixer with a paddle attachment to cream the lime zest with the butter and caster sugar until very fluffy, then add the eggs one at a time and mix to combine. Add the flour-fruit-nut mixture and, once that is incorporated, add the jam and lime juice, and mix to an even batter.
4. Transfer to the lined baking tin, smooth the top and sprinkle with the demerara sugar. Bake in the centre of the oven for 30 minutes, turn the tin, then bake for another 25–30 minutes until the cake feels bouncy to the touch. Allow to cool in the tin before removing. You can store this cake at room temperature for about 3–4 days.

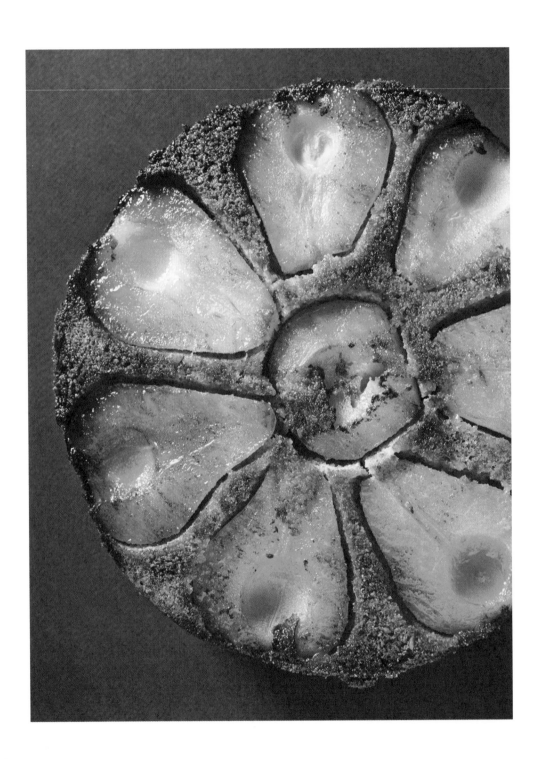

Pear and walnut upside-down cake

Pear and walnut is one of those winning combinations in the cookery world. Like liver and onion, or berries and cream, pears and walnuts bring out the best in each other: they share a slight astringency, a little sweetness, and a texture that is pleasantly grainy and buttery at the same time.

We go back to this combo a lot, as in the salad on page 78, or in this sweet variation on the theme: a polenta cake enriched with ground nuts and a hint of spice, topped with burnished, luscious fruit. Those of you who make this will be rewarded with a cake in autumnal shades of burnt amber and a kitchen full of delicate scent. It is a perfect companion for a chilly afternoon and a hot cup of something, or eat it with a dollop of rich cream as a lovely way to finish your meal.

Using polenta and nuts is an excellent alternative to using wheat flour, and with gluten branded the latest food enemy, this cake will make many people happy. There is one important thing to remember: when creaming the butter, beat it well enough that the sugar dissolves but not so much that it becomes all pale, as this will increase the chance of your cake sinking after it is baked.

Pear and walnut upside-down cake

Makes a 23-cm/9-inch round cake

For the topping (which starts life as the base)

4 small pears

60g/2¼oz/5 tbsp dark brown sugar

30g/1oz butter

For the cake batter

250g/9oz unsalted butter, at room temperature

300g/10½oz/1½ cups light brown sugar

4 medium eggs

175g/6oz/1¾ cups ground almonds

140g/5oz/scant 1½ cups ground walnuts (don't grind them too finely – a little texture is lovely here)

½ tsp ground nutmeg

1 tsp ground cinnamon

zest and juice of 1 orange

150g/5¼oz/1 cup easy-cook polenta

1 tsp baking powder

a pinch of salt (you could use salted butter instead)

1. Heat your oven to 180°C/160°C fan/350°F/gas mark 4.
2. Line the cake tin with baking paper – up the sides as well as over the base if you are using a loose-based tin, as the melting sugar will try and escape. Or you could just line the base and use some aluminium foil to wrap the outside of the tin to catch any leakage.
3. Peel and halve the pears, and use a teaspoon or melon baller to remove the pips.
4. Sprinkle the sugar for the topping on the base of the tin. Cut the butter into eight small pieces and place one in each pear, in the cavity created by scooping out the pips. Put the pear halves cut-side down on the bottom of the tin (so that the butter is touching the sugar) in a flower formation – seven 'petals' around the edges and one in the middle. You may need to trim the pears a little so that they fit snugly.
5. Use a mixer with a paddle attachment or a large spatula to cream the butter and sugar for the cake batter until well combined but not too fluffy. Add two of the eggs and mix well, then add the remaining ingredients (including the other two eggs) and beat together until you have a smooth batter. Spoon all over the pears to cover them entirely and use the back of a spoon to smooth the mixture out as much as possible. Bake in the centre of the oven for 30 minutes before rotating the tin to ensure an even bake, and continue baking for a further 20–25 minutes. (This cake is a little tricky: the texture will feel rather soft when it comes out, but it will settle and firm up after 20 minutes' cooling. My recommendation is to check the bake after the suggested times. The best way to tell if it has had long enough is to poke the edges, then poke the centre; they should feel the same. If your finger sinks immediately, add another 10 minutes to the baking time.)
6. Once it is done, remove from the oven and leave to cool in the tin (if you try and turn it out straight away, it will collapse). Wait 20 minutes (set a timer), then take a serving plate and place it on top of the baking tin. Flip the cake over and ease it out. Peel away the baking paper and serve. It is lovely warm but of course will keep well at room temperature too.

Summer weekends

We all travel, and as we do, we learn to accept certain truths about eating in the world: if you want the Parisian waiter to be nice to you, don't order the cheapest bottle; if you want a good coffee in Rome, go where the locals go; if you have the seafood paella, you had best prepare for the consequences. The restaurant with the spectacular view? The food will be awful, and if it isn't, you can be pretty sure that the bill will be.

We are citizens of the world, we are sophisticated and smart. In our travels we learn the ways of the world, and we accept them. We use them to our advantage. The Parisian waiter will defrost before our eyes as we order a bottle of Château Trop Cher from the bottom of the list; he will look after us, and we will have a grand night with great wine to go with it; or we can watch him stiffen and shrug as we order the first one on the list, and not give a damn about it. This is just how it works.

But sometimes it isn't. Sometimes that Parisian waiter will cosset you with attention, making sure you have a great time, despite your poor taste in wine – it'll be the most memorable night of your trip. Sometimes you will have seafood paella that will be good enough, fresh enough, to restore your faith in shellfish and in Spain. And just by Piazza Navona, where it seems no native Roman has been for centuries, there is an espresso bar that'll serve you as good a cup as any you could have in that city. We are wizened travellers, we are thick-skinned and ready, but when these things happen, we soften. We let our guard down. We are reminded why we love to travel in the first place.

A day at the beach on a Greek island. We are tired from the sun and salt, and hungry now. A wrong turn, a road on a cliff's edge, a sign: Taverna. We park and go in. The view takes our breath away: green island, blue sea, golden light, silver reflections. The food will be awful; we are ready for that, but we don't care. We have had a good day and we are here now, so we'll take in the views, and eat what we are given. Another bad sign: laminated menus. An endless list of dishes: Greek classics, burgers, pizza… a tourist trap. There is one other table occupied by a big group: kids, grandmas, a whole family – that of the owners, we think. They feel at home. Someone brings a pot from the kitchen to their table. A bit of commotion. We watch: bread is being rubbed with garlic and placed in a bowl; the contents of the pot are being ladled on top of it. The smell of garlic and mountain herbs is everywhere, the smell of meat and wine, sea and forest and sun. We ask our waiter what are they having. 'Stifado. It's rabbit.'
'Can we have some?'

Rabbit stifado

Serves 6

6 rabbit legs

**For the salt rub
(2–24 hours before cooking)**

2–3 sprigs each of thyme, sage and
rosemary, leaves picked

1 tbsp table salt

1 garlic clove, peeled

For cooking

3 long shallots, peeled and
cut into thick rings (about
2cm/¾ inch thick)

1 garlic clove, peeled and
halved lengthways

1 tbsp olive oil

200ml/7fl oz/scant 1 cup
dry white wine

1 tin chopped tomatoes
(400g/14oz)

1 tsp smoked paprika

1 tsp sweet paprika

1 tsp dried oregano

½ tsp freshly ground black pepper

1 tsp ground coriander

2–3 sprigs each of thyme, sage
and rosemary, tied together
with some string

To serve

toasted sourdough bread

1 garlic clove, peeled and halved

1. Finely chop the herbs and garlic for the rub, then mix into the salt (or you can pulse everything together in a small food processor, if you prefer). Rub all over the rabbit legs, then cover them and place in the fridge for at least 2 hours, or longer if you can – up to 24 hours, to intensify the herby flavour.

2. When you are ready to cook, heat your oven to 220°C/200°C fan/ 425°F/gas mark 7. Transfer the rabbit legs to a deep roasting pan or casserole that can fit them in one layer. Add the shallot rings and halved garlic clove. Drizzle with the olive oil and place in the hot oven for 10 minutes. Pour over the white wine and return to the oven for another 10 minutes. In the meantime, mix 500ml/18fl oz/2 cups of water with the tomatoes and dried spices.

3. Add the bouquet of fresh herbs to the roasting pan, pour the tomato liquid over everything and cover. Reduce the heat to 180°C/160°C fan/ 350°F/gas mark 4 and braise for 45 minutes. Remove from the oven and baste all over with the sauce. If you want, you can carefully flip the legs too. Re-cover and return to the oven for another 30 minutes. Remove to baste and flip again.

4. The cooking time will vary slightly, depending on how long you salted the meat, so the best way to check that it is done is to try a small bit of the rabbit. If it is soft, you are ready to serve; if not, return it to the oven for another 15 minutes before serving. If you are using wild rabbit, you will need to add another 30 minutes to the cooking time, and another basting too, to keep it moist. Serve with crusty toasted or griddled sourdough bread, rubbed with raw garlic.

Pickled peach salad with pistachios and parsley

We spend the summer months hunting for the perfect peach. It is a very satisfying pastime and one with delicious results. We get three boxes of peaches daily at the restaurant all through the season, and we check each one individually. The ones that look and smell perfect and have a slight give, but not too much, when you press them; these are the ones that are good to eat right now. These are the ones that we and our chefs get excited about, and these are the ones we serve to our customers as part of a simple starter with some crunchy lettuce leaves, salted almonds and goat's cheese, all lightly dressed with orange-blossom vinaigrette. When the fruit is at peak condition, it is hard to improve on this dish as a seasonal starter.

The ones that are a bit overripe will find their use as well – delicious peach jams and compôtes to serve at breakfast, roasted with vanilla for a cake filling or topping, or frozen with elderflower syrup to make the freshest and sweetest sorbet. The harder, crunchy ones are also welcome in our kitchen. They are extra special to us as they have all the summery floral flavour of peach without the sweetness, and their firm bite makes them perfect for more savoury preparations, such as a last-minute addition to slow-cooked lamb stew, chopped into a herby salad with cucumber and yogurt, or, maybe best of all, these delicious pickles. They are wonderful as a pre-dinner nibble on their own, as an accompaniment to meaty or fishy roasts like chicken, guinea fowl, salmon or trout, or (for a more complex but not at all complicated option) try this light, refreshing salad any time of the day. The subtle anise touch from the fennel seed and tarragon gives the fruit an unexpected freshness, and the buttery pistachios lend a touch of richness to this worthy salad.

The home cook is unlikely to have the luxury of going through three boxes of peaches a day. More often than not, you don't know the quality of the fruit till you get it home and try it, but whether your peaches are perfect to eat, a bit over, or a bit under, you are in for a treat as long as you know what to do with them, because all peaches are perfect, at least until September.

Pickled peach salad with pistachios and parsley

As a starter for 4 or as a side to a main course for 8

4 slightly firm peaches

For the pickling liquid

200ml/7fl oz/scant 1 cup cider vinegar or rice wine vinegar

3 tbsp honey

1 tsp whole fennel seeds

½ tsp whole black peppercorns

½ tsp sea salt

3 sprigs of tarragon

For the salad

1 head of Little Gem lettuce, broken into leaves

60g/2¼oz washed lamb's lettuce or butterhead lettuce

3 sprigs of tarragon, leaves picked

1 small bunch of parsley, leaves picked

3 tbsp olive oil

100g/3½oz/¾ cup roasted pistachios, roughly chopped

a sprinkling of flaky sea salt

freshly ground black pepper, to taste

1. Wash your peaches and cut into thin segments – about 8–10 from each peach. Set in a large bowl. Warm the vinegar and 100ml/3½fl oz/ scant ½ cup of water with the honey, fennel seeds, whole peppercorns and salt in a small pan over a low heat until all the honey has dissolved. You want the mixture to be warm but not boiling. Add the tarragon sprigs to the liquid, then pour over the cut peaches. Let them sit at room temperature for 1 hour, then cover with cling film and transfer to the fridge for a minimum of 2 hours and a maximum of 24 hours before serving.

2. Scatter the Little Gem leaves, lamb's lettuce and herbs on a serving platter. Top with the peaches and some of the pickling liquid, then drizzle with the oil and sprinkle the pistachios all over. Finish with a little sea salt and pepper and serve immediately.

Cold tomato and basil soup with crispy pitta shards

A good, middle class pastime for the summer months is getting to know the different varieties of tomatoes that are available now: datterino come in many sizes and colours, the small ones are the nicest – pop in the mouth like candy; spagnoletta are the crinkly ones that melt into the most delicious sauce; long fiery tubes of San Marzano – the Gucci of tomatoes – are good for everything.

We spotted some lovely tomatoes at a high-end grocer's and got a bit over-excited. For a small fortune we got a brown bagful that we arranged in the fruit bowl – tomatoes do not like refrigeration. We had some plans for them, but life (i.e. work) as always got in the way. By the end of the week they were too far gone, or almost too far. Good tomatoes never go to waste. There are things you can do with tomatoes that are just on the cusp, too soft for chopping, roasting or grilling but perfectly placed to collapse into a sauce or stew. On a hot day at the end of a long, hot week we made this – light and refreshing but exploding with summer's sweetness. The crisp pitta bits make it just substantial enough to be a good lunch. It is best to marinate all the ingredients together overnight for maximum flavour, so, if possible, start making this the day before you want to serve it.

A starter for 4 or a light summer lunch for 2

For the soup
8 very ripe plum tomatoes, quartered
1 small bunch of basil, leaves picked
3 garlic cloves, peeled
3 tbsp red wine vinegar
2 tbsp brown sugar
3 tbsp olive oil, plus more to serve
1 tsp sea salt, plus more to taste
1 tsp sweet paprika
4 ice cubes, plus more to serve

For the crispy pitta shards
2 pitta breads
2 tbsp olive oil
1 garlic clove, peeled and halved
½ tsp chilli flakes
1 tsp dried oregano

1. Put all the soup ingredients (apart from the ice) in a large jar or a deep bowl and mix well. Cover and set in the fridge overnight (or for at least 6 hours).
2. The following day, remove from the fridge, add the ice cubes and use a stick blender to blitz everything together to a smooth soup. Taste for seasoning – you may need another pinch of salt.
3. To make the crispy pitta, heat your oven to 190°C/170°C fan/375°F/ gas mark 5 and halve each pitta horizontally into two round discs. Brush both sides of the pitta discs with the olive oil and then rub all over with the halved garlic. Using a sharp, serrated knife, cut into long, thin strips.
4. Place these on a baking tray and bake for 10 minutes. Remove from the oven, sprinkle with the chilli flakes, oregano and a little sea salt and return to the oven until golden all over – it will take another 5–10 minutes.
5. Serve the soup with some extra ice, the crispy shards and a drizzling of olive oil.

Cold yogurt and pomegranate soup

You have to love a London scorcher – when the sun comes out, it shines a light on a city you didn't know existed: a sunny, seaside town, laid back and easy, every patch of grass filled with sun worshippers, bottles of rosé on pavement tables. Even the grey old Thames glistens in something resembling blue. Tables and chairs appear on every tiny patio and the humblest roof terrace turns into a riad rooftop – a place to have a sunny breakfast or to while away the warm evening with a cold drink.

We get a glimpse of the capital it could have been. If only this island were a few degrees further south.

But it isn't, of course. We do not have the infrastructure to deal with the heat: our terraced apartments are built to keep out the cold; our sash windows never fully open. And while the heat is great if you are in, say, Victoria Park, it is quite a different story if you are on a Victoria line train at 6pm in a car full of sweaty, crankier-than-usual commuters. By the time you get home you're as cranky as the rest of them. You are thirsty and hungry, but the mere thought of cooking or eating a hot dinner makes you break into sweat. Something fruity and cool is exactly what is called for, something that will not require an oven or a stove.

A small watermelon with some feta and olives would be great. Or, if you are lucky enough to find them, a punnet of tiny, sweet, new-season cucumbers; all you need do is dip them in olive oil and sea salt. However, if you are not completely beaten by the sun, try this cheeky little number: you can call it a chilled soup with crunchy vegetables or a chopped salad with a lot of dressing. It requires a bit of squeezing and dicing, but not a lot, and no cooking is involved. You'll be rewarded with a dish full of flavour and texture from the yogurt, herbs and fruit, a bit of a kick from the chilli and radishes, and a lot of pretty summer colours. Just the ticket to cool you down and fill you up, or as a great dinner party starter.

A summer starter for 4

For the soup

450ml/15½fl oz/2 cups runny goat's yogurt or 350ml/12fl oz/ 1½ cups normal goat's yogurt diluted with 100ml/3½fl oz/ scant ½ cup milk

½ tsp ground coriander

100ml/3½fl oz/scant ½ cup pomegranate juice (I press pomegranate halves through a sieve)

1 small garlic clove, peeled and minced or finely grated

4 tbsp olive oil

4 tbsp red wine vinegar or sherry vinegar

½ tsp salt

a generous pinch of cayenne pepper or a few drops of Tabasco

For the garnish

1 red chilli, thinly sliced

1 small bunch of red seedless grapes, halved

1 small punnet of cherry tomatoes, sliced

6–8 radishes, thinly sliced

seeds from ½ pomegranate

1 small handful of mint leaves, roughly chopped

1 small handful of coriander leaves, roughly chopped

To finish

a few ice cubes (optional – but great on a hot day)

a drizzle of olive oil

1. Mix all the soup ingredients together and set in the fridge to chill for at least 30 minutes.

2. When you are ready to serve, half-fill each serving bowl with soup and top with a little of everything from the list of garnishes, plus a couple of ice cubes and a drizzle of olive oil. Alternatively, you can lay everything out on the table and let people choose their own toppings. Serve with a crusty loaf of bread and lots of sunshine.

Sardines with roasted tomatoes and crispy pitta

It felt like the thing to do – head to a Greek island. A small villa on a verdant hillside, ours for a week. We would spend lazy days on the beach and nip down to the pretty little village for glorious sun-sweet ingredients – those lovely tomatoes, the freshest fish, that famous olive oil, country bread, peaches. Cooking would be an absolute pleasure, and dining on our balcony an even bigger one. After a busy summer in the very hot, stressful kitchen of our London restaurant, it seemed an extremely appealing idea.

The island, the hillside, our little villa – perfect. Quite a basic kitchen, but it would do, and the beach and the water were heaven. The village was even cuter than the pictures online (when does this ever happen?). The vegetables and the fish looked as good as we imagined them; we always wish for produce like this back in London…

When we got back to the house with our shopping – hungry as only a day on the beach can make you, covered in sea salt, woozy from the sudden sun and from our exhausting summer – we realised that the last thing either of us wanted to do on our holiday was stand in the kitchen and cook.

But dinner had to be made: there were sardines in the fridge that were too good to go to waste, no matter how tired we were. The following dish is what we cooked, if cooking is not too big a word for it – bread and oil in a tray in the oven, then tomatoes and fish chucked on top a bit later with only essential seasoning: garlic, a few sprigs of thyme from the driveway, some salt and plenty of that famous olive oil. Sardines on toast essentially, Greek-fashion.

We got the balcony dinner of our dreams: salty fish and sweet tomatoes, some bits of bread, soggy and full of flavour from the pan sauce, some still crisp. The sun setting on the sea below and the breeze blowing. No Greek god could have had a better evening.

We didn't cook much after that. We had our dinners in the local taverna and spent the rest of our holiday evenings with our podcasts, our Bruce Chatwin and our backgammon board. We had a big year coming. Someone else could do the cooking for a week.

Sardines with roasted tomatoes and crispy pitta

Light dinner for 2

For the crispy pitta

2 tbsp olive oil

1 pitta bread

a sprinkling of sea salt

For the fish

500g/1lb 2oz small tomatoes

4 garlic cloves, peeled and halved

4–5 sprigs of thyme

4 butterflied sardines (you can keep whole if you prefer)

3 tbsp olive oil

1 tsp sea salt

1 tsp sugar

1. Heat your oven to 220°C/200°C fan/425°F/gas mark 7. Pour the olive oil for the crispy pitta in a large casserole, oven-proof frying pan or roasting tin. Rip the pitta into bite-sized pieces, toss in the oil, sprinkle with the salt and place in the oven for 6–8 minutes, or until the pitta shards start to colour.

2. Remove the pan from the oven and top with the tomatoes, garlic and thyme, then top with the butterflied sardines, skin-side up. Drizzle everything with the olive oil and sprinkle with the salt and sugar.

3. Return to the oven for 10 minutes, then serve immediately.

Frozen tahini parfait and chocolate sandwich cake

'Have nothing in your house that you do not know to be useful, or believe to be beautiful.' Easier said than done, Mr. Morris, especially when you share the house you live in. We each have our own definition of what we think useful and believe beautiful, and there's a tremendous amount of stuff to consider…

In our house there are just the two of us. A decade plus of living together has taught us to choose our battles very carefully, and even if we disagree about what is handsome and/or handy, sometimes it is better just to leave it.

Our home is dotted with these fault lines, little mementos of conversations we decided not to finish, lest they disturb the domestic peace. A little table that cracked last year; I want to have it fixed; she wants to throw it away; for now, it is just there. When we couldn't decide on bedside lights, we just went without for three years. I surprised her recently with a pair of jet-black anglepoise lamps, beautifully formed and highly functional. I thought, 'Nice'.

She said, 'I always wanted my bedroom to look like a World War II interrogation room.'

'Not a fan', I think.

But, like most couples, we tend to agree on most things (the big things, at least) and we always love having this dessert in the house. We find it beautiful, both to look at (with the pretty marbling of the date syrup in the parfait) and to eat (with its smooth texture and gentle, nutty sweetness). We both think it's a very useful thing to have in the house. You can make it well in advance and pull it out of the freezer when people visit, and, unless you are having a very large party over, you are almost guaranteed to have leftovers to put back in the freezer. For the next lot of guests, or just when you fancy a little sweet something.

Frozen tahini parfait and chocolate sandwich cake

Fills a 23-cm/9-inch round cake tin

For the chocolate sponge

butter, for greasing

4 eggs, separated

120g/4¼oz/⅔ cup caster sugar

50ml/1¾fl oz/3½ tbsp milk

30g/1oz/⅓ cup cocoa powder

50g/1¾oz/6 tbsp plain flour

For the tahini parfait

600g/1lb 5oz/2¾ cups double cream

150g/5¼oz/⅔ cup tahini paste

100g/3½oz/½ cup + 1 tbsp caster sugar

3 tbsp date molasses

For the chocolate glaze

100g/3½oz/½ cup double cream

1 tbsp date molasses

100g/3½oz dark chocolate of your choice

1. Heat your oven to 190°C/170°C fan/375°F/gas mark 5. Meanwhile, line two 23-cm/9-inch round cake tins with a circle of baking paper in each base and lightly butter the sides.

2. Whisk the egg whites in a large mixer bowl with a whisk attachment until they start to foam. Continue to whisk while slowly adding half the sugar, until you have a nice fluffy meringue.

3. In a separate bowl mix the egg yolks with the milk, then add the remaining 60g/2¼oz/⅓ cup of sugar, the cocoa powder and the flour and combine until you have a smooth paste.

4. Take a spoonful of meringue and stir into the paste to loosen it, then fold the paste into the remaining meringue, trying to keep in as much air as possible. Divide the batter between your prepared tins and bake for 10–12 minutes. The sponge should just feel bouncy, and when you lightly touch it with the tip of your finger, it should come away dry. Allow to cool in the tins.

5. Whisk the cream, tahini and sugar for the parfait together in a mixing bowl on a low speed until it thickens to a rich, soft, whipped cream. Scoop onto one of the sponges in its tin and spread around to cover the entire base. Now use a spoon to drizzle the date molasses all around in swirling motions, so it creates a lovely pattern on the cream. You can make the swirls more pronounced by using the handle of the spoon to swirl the molasses deeper into the cream.

6. Lift the second sponge out of its tin and flip it sponge-side-down onto the parfait (the baking paper will be on top now). Pop into the freezer for a minimum of 2 hours, and up to a month, before glazing.

7. When you come to remove the frozen sandwich-cake from the tin, use a cloth soaked in hot water to wipe the sides of the tin to warm them slightly (or use a blow torch, as they do in professional kitchens). Tip or lift the cake out (depending on whether or not you are using a loose-based tin) and peel the baking paper off the top and bottom before placing on a serving plate. Return to the freezer until you are ready to glaze.

8. Heat the cream and date molasses to boiling point in a small pan, then pour over the chopped chocolate in a bowl and stir till smooth and shiny. Pour onto the top sponge and use the back of a spoon to spread in lovely waves to cover. Don't worry if some drizzles off the sides – it will look really tempting. Serve now, or return it to the freezer till you are ready.

Frozen meringue bar with strawberry and lime

Is this a bit retro? Maybe, but this dessert should never go out of fashion. It is lighter than light, made mostly of air held together by a delicate, freshly flavoured foam. Bring this one out at the end of a big meal, and when everyone says, 'Oh, I couldn't possibly', you'll soon discover that, actually, they can. You need to make it ahead as it takes time to set, but once made, you can store it in the freezer for up to a month and, as long as it is covered, it will keep well. The strawberries also benefit from sitting in their marinade for at least a few hours. We used a loaf tin here, but it'd look great in a round tin or a silicone bundt.

Fills a 1-kg/2lb 4-oz loaf tin or a similar-capacity silicone mould of your choosing

For the frozen meringue

3 egg whites (about 120g/4¼oz)

130g/4½oz/⅔ cup sugar

240g/8½oz/generous 1 cup double cream

zest of 2 limes

For the macerated strawberries

350g/12⅓oz/3½ cups strawberries

5 tbsp sugar

juice of 1 lime

flesh of 1 lime

1 tbsp rose water

2 tbsp gin or vodka

1. You will need to start preparing this at least a day before serving. Line your loaf tin with a large piece of cling film, allow some overhang down the sides to ease lifting out later. You can use a sheet of baking paper if you prefer (if you are using a silicone mould, it will not require any lining at all).

2. Whisk the egg whites with the sugar until they form really stiff peaks. In a separate bowl whip the cream with the lime zest to soft peaks. Fold the two mixtures together, then transfer to the prepared tin. Fold the film overhang to cover the top (or cover with cling film if using a silicone mould) and place in the coldest section of the freezer for at least 10 hours.

3. You can macerate the strawberries a day in advance if you wish, or just a few hours before serving. Wash and hull them, then cut into quarters. Combine with all the macerating ingredients in a bowl, cover and place in the fridge until needed.

4. Once you are ready to serve (you need to do this bit at the last minute), remove the tin from the freezer, peel back the covering and use the overhang to help you lift the frozen meringue out. Now place it on a plate and peel off the lining.

5. Top with the strawberries and serve the remaining liquid on the side, so people can add as much as they want.

Baked custard fruit tart

You can look down on custard powder if you like, but we aren't food snobs, and every home baker worth his or her salt – or sugar – knows it's a handy little number to have in the kitchen. Add a bit to shortbread or cake mixtures for a bit of childhood-flavoured magic, or use it to make this excellent tart filling.

There is no cream or milk in this, unlike a 'normal' custard tart. Instead it has a rich, baked buttercream.

The recipe below yields enough pastry to make two tarts. You could halve it, but I always think that recipes with just half an egg are extremely annoying. Make the full amount, split it in two and freeze half for a future date. Or bake two tarts now. You can never have enough tart.

To fill a long, narrow, rectangular loose-based tart tin or an 18-cm/7-inch round tart tin

For the sweet pastry (enough for 2 tarts)

250g/9oz/1¾ cups + 2 tbsp flour

130g/4½oz/scant 1 cup icing sugar

110g/4oz butter

1 egg

zest of 1 lemon

For the filling (enough for 1 tart)

45g/1½oz/5 tbsp icing sugar

50g/1¾oz soft butter

2 egg yolks

3 tbsp custard powder

a pinch of salt

1 tbsp peach schnapps or brandy

peaches and/or apricots, or really any fruit you fancy that has some sharpness (rhubarb, plums, raspberries – they all work)

a little sugar, for sprinkling

1. Mix all the pastry ingredients together to form a dough. You can use a mixer with a paddle attachment or a food processor if you wish, but mixing it by hand will work just as well.
2. Divide the pastry in two and freeze one half for next time (if you are only making one tart now). Wrap the other half in cling film and rest in the fridge for at least half an hour.
3. Lightly flour your work surface and roll out the pastry. Lift into the tin and make sure to push right into the corners, then trim the edges. There is no need to blind-bake this tart, as the time it takes to bake the filling will be enough to crisp up the pastry.
4. Heat your oven to 190°C/170°C fan/375°F/gas mark 5. Place all the filling ingredients in a food processor and work together until really smooth and well-combined. Spread the filling on the base of the tart: it should fill it just under halfway. It may not seem like much, but it grows as it bakes.
5. Now arrange the fruit however you like. You can halve the apricots and quarter or segment the peaches, and stand them up in the filling (cut-side upwards) in alternating rows like little soldiers. Sprinkle with a little bit of sugar and bake in the oven for 15 minutes. Rotate the tin and bake for a further 15 minutes. The filling should have become slightly golden and firmed up. Remove from the oven and cool in the tin before removing and slicing.

For a crowd

Our own wedding party, it has to be said, was more than a bit chaotic, prescient perhaps of the crazy energy that would typify our life together. We had eloped and got married in Cyprus (or at least we tried to elope – our families followed on a privately chartered plane and ended up attending the charming little ceremony that marked our beginning), but we wanted, on our return, to throw a party for our nearest and dearest.

We had the romantic, very naïve notion that we could do it all ourselves. We took over Sarit's parents' house: the big garden would comfortably fit the hundred or so guests we had invited; Hazel's well-stocked kitchen had everything we needed; and the neighbour had offered extra fridge space, just in case. We had great fun deciding on the menu and even more fun getting the produce from the Turkish market in Haifa. We hired a local DJ who had strange taste in music, and we got some friends to drop by and help us prep. Our closest chef friends were assigned to kitchen duty. On the evening, even as guests started to arrive, when most brides would be finishing their hair and make-up, my bride was in the kitchen, giving the desserts a final touch.

It was not a perfect night. The bride and groom spent most of it in the kitchen, avoiding attention, hiding from relatives and small talk. The power kept tripping, the music was weird, but it was, in its way, perfect for us. We would not have had it any other way. Our life together began just as it would continue, with us two in the kitchen, trying to make life a celebration. Living in restaurants is like throwing a party every night.

We know how to throw a party now. During wedding season, we cater for a big party almost every week, mostly weddings. Holly and Alex loved coming to Honey & Co, so when they decided to get married, they asked us to cater the event. Louisa, who handles our catering (we call her the bride-whisperer), pored over every detail with them, e-mails going back and forth for months discussing menus (and amending them), equipment hire, ice deliveries, drinks and who would serve them. All so that on a beautiful summer day, in a disused church next to a south London park, the right wine was served at the right temperature at the right time; the kitchen, which we set up in what was essentially a broom cupboard, was able seamlessly to send out beautiful food for a hundred people; and, in the middle of it all, two happy people in a beautiful room were surrounded by the people they love, celebrating love and life and hope.

In another converted church, this one on a suburban street in north west London, Gavin and Magnolia also have much to celebrate: they turned the church into a magnificent family home; with its high, vaulted ceiling and stained-glass windows, the place is always party-ready. We know their house well by now – we catered their house-warming party the first year, their wedding party the next, and their child's first birthday a couple of years after that. We know the food they like to serve and the plates they like to use. We know where everything is in the kitchen and what to do with the leftover food and the waste at the end of the night.

The parties we throw ourselves still tend to be rushed, ad hoc affairs. We'll get to the end of December and realise we have forgotten to have a staff party, and we'll whip something together. Or, as our work requires us from time to time to cook large amounts of food at home, we'll invite over whoever we meet. There are never enough chairs and usually too much food, but it's always good fun.

On other occasions, we enjoy planning and executing a special feast for a special someone or a worthy occasion. We take great care with the food, obviously, but also with the flowers, the music and everything else, taking our time and finding great pleasure in the details, pausing to appreciate the things in life that are worth celebrating.

Smoked haddock doughnuts

The longer you stay in one place, the harder it is to move. The contents of our little Brixton flat were packed into a surprising number of boxes, even after a major cull. So we moved our little household, which consists of us two, a suicidal yucca plant and a cheery cheese plant, which refuses to die despite our best efforts. We didn't travel far, only a few roads up to Stockwell, but whatever the distance, the hassle of setting up a new home is considerable: deliveries and trade people to coordinate, the dread of being without Wi-Fi for a few days, the inevitable trip to Ikea, the meatballs, the inevitable second trip to Ikea to replace and return things, more meatballs... Knowing the drill doesn't make it any easier but in a way, all this activity served to distract us from the fact that we had left behind a place that was full of very happy memories for us. But eventually it catches up with you, when the boxes are unpacked and the pictures are hanging, when you find yourself at the end of the day in a new place surrounded by familiar furniture, wondering what kind of memories will be made between these walls.

We are all settled now. The cheese plant has unfurled three new leaves since we moved; the yucca keeps toppling over, as it always does; and we go about filling the place with storage solutions, occasional furniture, and bathroom accessories. And getting our house-warming party going, because nothing fills a house with good memories like nice food and nice people.

These little nuggets are perfect party food: savoury and just salty enough to get you reaching for your drink; easy to pass around and pick up. The batter can be made well in advance but you do need to serve them fresh from the pan – an excuse for the host to spend some time getting to know their new kitchen.

Makes 25–30 little doughnuts for a party, or enough slightly larger ones for a starter for 6

2 potatoes (about 500–600g/ 1lb 2–5oz raw)

250g/9oz smoked haddock

250ml/8¾fl oz/generous 1 cup milk

2 bay leaves

½ tsp whole peppercorns

50g/1¾oz unsalted butter

100g/3½oz/¾ cup plain flour

½ tsp salt, plus more to taste, if needed

1 large egg

1 garlic clove, peeled and crushed (or more, if you love garlic)

vegetable oil, for frying

To serve (optional)

tomato wedges

lemon wedges

parsley leaves, picked

a good sprinkle of sea salt

Smoked haddock doughnuts

1. Heat the oven to 220°C/200°C fan/425°F/gas mark 7. Place the potatoes directly on the oven rack and bake till cooked through and slightly charred on the outside. This will take 45–60 minutes, depending on their size. Check they're done by inserting a knife – it should go in easily.

2. In the meantime, place the fish, milk, bay leaves and peppercorns in a pan, bring to the boil and then simmer for a minute till the fish is just cooked (if they are thick pieces it may take 30 seconds longer). Remove from the heat and leave in the pan for 30 minutes or so, to allow the flavours to infuse. Remove the fish from the pan gently – a spatula would come in handy. Strain the milk into a small saucepan.

3. Add the butter to the milk and set on a low heat until the butter is melted. Mix the flour and the half teaspoon of salt together. Add all the seasoned flour to the pan in one go, and stir vigorously over the heat till the mixture comes together to a smooth ball. Transfer to a bowl. Stir in the egg. The paste will initially fall apart but keep mixing and it will come together again to a smooth, slightly wet dough.

4. Cut the potatoes in half and scoop the flesh into the dough. Flake the fish and add it too, along with the crushed garlic. Fold in gently so as not to break up the fish and potato too much. Now taste the mixture – it may need some extra salt, but it will depend on how salty your smoked haddock is.

5. In a deep frying pan heat about 5cm/2 inches of vegetable oil. When the oil is hot enough (check it by popping a pinch of the mixture in – it should fizz up), use a spoon to scoop up some mixture, and another spoon to push it into the oil. The balls should sizzle as soon as they hit the oil. Repeat till the pan is full. Fry for two minutes till the undersides are golden brown, then flip them gently with a spoon. Once the other side is nicely coloured, remove from the pan and place on a plate lined with absorbent kitchen paper. Now fry the next batch. It will probably take 3–4 batches, depending on the size of your pan.

6. Place on a serving platter with tomato and lemon wedges, parsley leaves and a sprinkle of sea salt. Eat as soon, and as many, as you can.

Taramosalata

Finding tarama fish roe isn't the easiest thing, but a good fishmonger or Greek deli should have it in stock. Make sure not to buy the ready-made taramosalata dip but instead get the salted, cured roe, so that you can make your own dip and discover how delicious it can be.

For nibbles for 8–10 at a party or a starter for 4–6

50g/1¾oz crustless sourdough bread

100ml/3½fl oz/scant ½ cup milk (or water, if you are avoiding diary)

120g/4¼oz tarama (salted and cured fish roe)

1 large garlic clove, peeled and minced

350ml/12fl oz/1½ cups vegetable oil

juice of ½ lemon (or less, to taste)

To serve

a selection of dippers, such as radishes, carrots and celery

slices of crusty bread

1. Put the bread in a mixer with a paddle attachment or in a food processor. Pour in the milk and leave the bread to soak for about 10 minutes.
2. Once the bread has softened, add the tarama and garlic, and mix or blitz until it forms a thick, smooth paste. Slowly add the oil in a steady drizzle, mixing all the time, until fully incorporated. Finish by adding as much of the lemon juice as you want, to taste. You can thin the dip with a touch of milk or water if it is too thick for your liking. Serve with some crispy dippers like radishes, carrots or celery, and some nice, crusty bread.

Kamunia (a different kind of chopped liver)

This may not be what you think of when you think of chopped liver, but it should be. The deep, earthy flavour of fried liver gets a lift and kick here from cumin, lemon and as much chilli heat as you like – it can take it with class.

For nibbles for 8–10 at a party or as a starter for 4–6

For the onions

2 tbsp vegetable oil

3 onions, peeled and sliced

1 tsp sugar

For the liver

1 tbsp vegetable oil

30g/1oz butter

300g/10½oz fresh chicken livers, cleaned of any sinew or veins

½ tsp salt

¼ tsp freshly ground black pepper

1 tbsp ground cumin

juice of ½ lemon

1 tbsp Turkish acı biber salçası pepper paste, or mix 1 tsp smoked paprika and 1 tsp sweet paprika with 2 tsp vegetable oil

To serve (optional)

boiled eggs, sliced

Turkish chilli flakes

halved radishes

pickled cucumbers

crackers or cholla

1. Heat the oil and sliced onions in a large frying pan on a medium heat and cook for 20–25 minutes, or until really reduced and starting to brown. Add the sugar and mix well, then cook for a further 5 minutes until dark brown. Remove to a bowl on the side.
2. Using the same frying pan, heat the oil and butter for the liver. Fry the livers on all sides and season with the salt and pepper. Then, just as they colour all over to a lovely golden brown, add the cumin, lemon juice and pepper paste, and mix well to coat. Return the onions to the pan and stir everything together, then remove to a bowl to cool.
3. Once the liver is cold enough to handle, transfer to a chopping board and roughly chop before placing on a serving platter. Garnish with sliced boiled eggs and sprinkle with some chilli flakes. Serve with radishes, pickled cucumbers and some bread or crackers.

Pumpkin chirshi

This dip originates from the Maghreb region of North Africa. The sweetness of the pumpkin and the heat from the spices work together like a dream. You can serve it as a dip on its own or as a delicious relish, which goes with pretty much anything – although roast fish and seafood are big favourites of ours. Any leftovers are guaranteed to give the next day's sandwich an incredible lift.

For nibbles for 8–10 at a party or as a starter for 4–6

For the pumpkin purée

2kg/4lb 8oz raw pumpkin, cut into large wedges (skin on)

For the chirshi

4 tbsp olive oil

4 garlic cloves, peeled

1 tsp ground caraway

1 tsp ground cumin

1 tsp sweet paprika

a pinch of ground cinnamon

2 tsp harissa paste

700g/1lb 9oz/generous 3 cups pumpkin purée (see above)

1 tsp salt

1 tbsp honey

1 small bunch of coriander, chopped

1. If possible, make the pumpkin purée the evening before you want to make the chirshi. Heat your oven to 220°C/200°C fan/425°F/gas mark 7. Place the pumpkin wedges on a baking tray, flesh-side up, and roast for about 30–40 minutes or until the flesh is very soft. Remove from the oven and cool a little until you can handle the wedges easily. Use a spoon to scoop all the flesh off the skin and into a fine sieve. Set over the sink to drain any excess water for at least 2 hours, or ideally overnight.
2. The following day, heat the oil in a large frying pan on a medium-low heat and cook the garlic until soft but not brown. Stir in the spices and fry for another minute before adding the pumpkin purée, salt and honey. Cook for 5–6 minutes, stirring occasionally to make sure it doesn't stick, then add the chopped coriander to the warm purée. Mix well and transfer to a serving dish.

Fennel crackers with arak and sugar

Is there a point in making crackers at home when you can get such nice ones pretty much everywhere? The answer depends on how much time you have and your level of commitment. If you do choose to make your own, make it count. These are unlike anything you can buy in the shops – savoury, sweet and crisp, with a note of anise that does not overpower.

Makes 12

350g/12⅓oz strong white bread flour, plus more for dusting

50g/1¾oz sugar

10g/⅓oz/2 tsp salt

30g/1oz fresh yeast or 15g/½oz dried active yeast

180–200ml/6¼–7fl oz/generous ¾ cup cold water

4–5 tbsp olive oil, for brushing

2 tbsp whole fennel seeds

a good sprinkling of caster sugar

50ml/1¾fl oz/3½ tbsp arak, raki or Pernod

1. You can use an electric mixer with a dough hook to make these, or mix by hand. Combine the flour, sugar and salt together, then crumble in the fresh yeast. If you are using dried yeast, dissolve it in a little of the water before adding to the flour.
2. Mix in the water gradually until the dough comes together to a ball. Increase the mixer speed and work for about 2–3 minutes (or continue working by hand) until the dough becomes elastic, shiny and pliable. Transfer to a lightly oiled bowl and place in the fridge to rest for at least one hour, and up to 24 hours.
3. Dust your work surface very lightly with flour and turn the dough out of the bowl. Use a knife or pastry cutter to cut into twelve even pieces (about 50g/1¾oz each). Roll each piece into a small, tight ball and lay on a tray dusted with some more flour. Cover the tray loosely with cling film or a cloth and leave to rest for about 30 minutes.
4. Heat your oven to 200°C/180°C fan/400°F/gas mark 6. Line two or three flat trays with baking paper.
5. Dust your work surface with a generous amount of flour and use a rolling pin to flatten each ball into an oval about 16–18cm/6¼–7 inches long. You can flip the dough over a couple of times to ease the rolling, but keep the shape if you can. Carefully transfer the rolled dough ovals to the lined trays.
6. Brush the ovals very lightly with olive oil before sprinkling on the fennel seeds so there are some on each one. Then sprinkle generously with caster sugar until there is a thin visible layer on top.
7. Bake for 8–10 minutes or until dark golden. Remove from the oven and use a brush to dab a tiny bit of arak onto the surface of each cracker. Return to the oven for another 2 minutes to dry.
8. Remove to a wire rack to cool and crisp. Store in an airtight container.

Harissa and goat's cheese buns

Make the dough for these in advance and leave the tray in the fridge. Preheat the oven, and pop them in when people start to arrive. The smell of these buns baking is enough to get the party going, and they are perfect served hot from the oven with a cold drink.

Makes about 20

175g/6oz/1⅓ cups self-raising flour

100g/3½oz butter (at room temperature), diced

1 egg, lightly whisked and divided into 2 small bowls

60g/2¼oz/generous ⅔ cup finely grated pecorino or Parmesan, divided into 2 small bowls

125g/4½oz/½ cup ricotta

125g/4½oz soft, young, rindless goat's cheese

30g/1oz/2 tbsp rose harissa paste

1 tsp sea salt or a generous pinch of table salt

1 tsp whole cumin seeds

1. I use a mixer to make these; the dough is easy enough to make by hand, but it's a little messy. Place the flour and butter in a mixer bowl with a paddle attachment and combine to a crumb-like consistency. Add half the egg and half the grated pecorino or Parmesan, along with the ricotta, goat's cheese, harissa paste and salt. Mix together until everything forms a nice, soft, pliable dough.
2. Divide the dough into two pieces and roll each one into a log about 20cm/8 inches long. Brush each log all over with the other half of the egg, which you set aside earlier.
3. Mix the remaining pecorino or Parmesan and the cumin seeds together, and sprinkle on the work surface. Roll the logs in the cheese-cumin mixture until coated all over. Place on a tray in the fridge to rest for at least an hour, and up to 48 hours.
4. When you are ready to bake – best done just before serving as these are great hot – heat your oven to 200°C/180°C fan/400°F/gas mark 6. Cut each log into about 10 slices, each about 2cm/¾ inch thick, and lay them flat on a lined baking tray. Bake for about 13–15 minutes until the cheese becomes golden but the buns are still soft. Remove from the oven and serve hot.

Kalamata olive and orange maamool

Another recipe inspired by the legendary Orna & Ella in Tel Aviv, where my kitchen life began. This has been a fixture on their canapé menu for years, as it now is in ours. In our kitchen, just as in theirs, the chefs flock when this comes out of the oven, eager for the trimmings.

Makes about 24–28

For the orange semolina dough

250g/9oz/1¾ cups plain flour, plus more for dusting

30g/1oz/4 tbsp semolina

1 tsp baking power

a pinch of salt

50ml/1¾fl oz/3½ tbsp olive oil

50ml/1¾fl oz/3½ tbsp vegetable oil

100ml/3½fl oz/scant ½ cup orange juice

For the olive filling

1 tsp dried tarragon

1 tsp dried oregano

½ tsp dried mint

zest of 1 orange

30g/1oz/⅓ cup grated pecorino

130g/4½oz/1⅓ cups pitted black Kalamata olives

a large pinch of cracked black pepper

olive oil, for brushing

1. Mix the flour with the semolina, baking powder and salt in a bowl. Add the oils and the orange juice and mix to form a light, even dough. Wrap in cling film and set aside at room temperature (do not chill) for 30 minutes.
2. Make the olive filling by blitzing all the ingredients together in a food processor.
3. Heat your oven to 200°C/180°C fan/400°F/gas mark 6 and line a flat tray with a sheet of baking paper.
4. Lightly dust the work surface with some flour and roll out the dough to a rectangle of about 20 x 30cm/8 x 11¾ inches, with the long edge closest to you. Scoop half the olive filling onto the bottom part of the rectangle and press down to flatten a little. Roll the dough over the filling to create a log. This should roughly reach the centre of the rolled-out sheet. Use a knife to cut the log off, leaving the remaining half of the rectangle on the work surface. Lift the log onto the tray and repeat the process with the remaining dough so that you have two olive-filled logs.
5. Bake for 15 minutes, then rotate the tray for an even bake, and add another 10 minutes to your timer. After this time, remove the logs and brush with olive oil, then return to the oven for a final 3 minutes.
6. Remove from the oven and allow to cool a little, then use a sharp knife to slice each log into 12–14 pieces.

Spiced butternut squash phylas

Makes about 20

1 packet of filo pastry

100g/3½oz melted butter

For the filling

4 tbsp olive oil

a 5-cm/2-inch cinnamon stick

1 small whole dried chilli or a pinch of chilli flakes

2 long shallots or 1 small red onion, peeled and chopped (about 100g/3½oz)

1 butternut squash (about 600–700g/1lb 5–9oz), peeled and grated (yielding about 500g/1lb 2oz)

a pinch of salt

1 tsp ground cumin

1 tsp ground coriander

6 sage leaves, finely chopped

1 tbsp honey

60g/2¼oz feta, crumbled

1. Heat the olive oil in a frying pan on a medium heat. Add the cinnamon stick and whole chilli or chilli flakes, followed by the chopped shallots or onion and fry for about 1 minute before adding the grated butternut squash and salt. Stir around and cook until the butternut softens. This will take about 10 minutes.

2. Stir in the ground cumin and coriander, then fry for 30 seconds before removing the pan from the heat. Add the chopped sage and honey, and mix well. Allow to cool before removing the cinnamon stick and whole dried chilli (if using), and stirring in the crumbled feta.

3. Heat your oven to 220°C/200°C fan/425°F/gas mark 7 and line a baking tray with baking paper.

4. Open the filo packet on the work surface and lay it so that the pastry is folded in half with the narrow end of the rectangle closest to you. Pull out two sheets at a time and brush the top sheet with melted butter. Spoon pumpkin filling in a thin line along the closest edge of the filo and roll up loosely to form a 'snake'. Cut away the unused pastry just above the 'snake'. Roll the 'snake' into a 'snail', tucking the end underneath, and place on the baking tray. Continue filling and rolling the remaining part of the filo until it is used up, then pull out a new pair of sheets and start again.

5. Repeat again and again until all the filling is used up. Brush the remaining butter on the tops of the phylas. You can now bake them for 12–14 minutes, or until golden all over. Alternatively, you can keep the 'snails' in the fridge for up to 24 hours before baking.

Roasted Romano peppers, chickpeas, olives, roasted tomatoes and cumin

Most of the food in our restaurants begins its life in our home kitchen, then travels to work to be recreated there. This dish made the reverse journey. The perennial star of the takeaway counter in Honey & Spice, it first came to life by accident in the heady days of opening the shop. Some leftover chickpeas; roasted peppers and tomatoes we had for making sandwiches; olives, parsley and cumin, which are always kicking around in our kitchen... the colours were there, the flavours were there. We make it every day now, and it is always the first dish to sell out during our short and violent lunchtime rush.

It made the journey home with ease as it is delicious, and even works well with tinned chickpeas. It's a useful little number to have as part of a buffet, or as a side dish to steal the show.

Makes enough salad for a party or for 8–10 as part of a spread

125g/4½oz/¾ cup dried chickpeas, soaked overnight in plenty of water (or 2 tins cooked chickpeas)

5 tbsp olive oil

1 tsp salt

2 tbsp ground cumin

4 garlic cloves, peeled and crushed

200g/7oz/1¼ cups cherry tomatoes

4–5 sprigs of thyme

a pinch of sugar

3 red Romano peppers

1 bunch of parsley, leaves picked

60g/2¼oz/⅔ cup Kalamata black olives, pitted and sliced

juice of 2 lemons

1. Drain the soaked chickpeas, then place in a pan and boil in plenty of fresh water until they are soft. This can take around an hour, so top up the water if it reduces too much. If you decide to use tinned chickpeas, drain them well, then place in a pan of fresh water and bring to the boil. Then continue as if you were using freshly cooked, even though nothing compares to cooking your own.

2. Drain the boiled chickpeas and, while they are still hot, season with two tablespoons of the olive oil, the salt, half the cumin and one of the crushed garlic cloves (keep the rest for later). Mix well, tip into a large serving bowl and leave to cool.

3. Place the cherry tomatoes in a frying pan with the remaining three tablespoons of olive oil, the thyme sprigs and the other three garlic cloves. Fry on a high heat till the tomatoes start exploding, then sprinkle with the sugar. Remove the garlic cloves and thyme springs, and pour the tomatoes and oil onto the chickpeas.

4. Roast the peppers in a very hot oven (240°C/220°C fan/475°F/gas mark 9) or directly over a gas flame until they are charred all over. Place them in a sealable plastic bag or a closed container to steam as they cool. When they are cool enough to handle, peel, deseed and tear into long strips. Add to the chickpea and tomato bowl.

5. Finally, just before serving, add the parsley, olives, the remaining tablespoon of ground cumin and the lemon juice. Mix well and serve.

Cherry, herb and freekeh tabule

Throughout the Middle East, freekeh is prepared in the spring. The wheat is picked while the sheaves are still green and the wheat kernels are still soft. The crops are harvested and arranged in piles to dry, and then are carefully set on fire to burn away the chaff and straw. The moisture in the wheat kernels prevents them from burning; they just take on a very subtle smokiness. Once cooled, the wheat is rubbed by hand (hence the name: farik means rubbed in Arabic), then dried and stored for use throughout the year.

Makes enough salad for a party or for 8–10 as part of a spread

For the freekeh

250g/9oz/1⅓ cups dried freekeh

2 celery sticks

1 carrot, peeled and halved lengthways

1 bay leaf

2 tbsp olive oil

1 tsp salt

For the salad

juice and zest of 1 lemon

1 small bunch of parsley, leaves picked and roughly chopped

1 small bunch of tarragon, leaves picked and roughly chopped

1 small bunch of mint, leaves picked and roughly chopped

60g/2¼oz/½ cup roasted pistachios, chopped

60g/2¼oz/scant ½ cup roasted almonds, chopped

300g/10½oz/2 cups cherries, pitted and quartered

1 celery heart, stalks finely chopped

1 tsp sea salt

3 tbsp olive oil

1. Rinse the freekeh under cold water, then place in a large pan and cover with 1 litre/1¾ pints/4⅓ cups of fresh water. Add the celery, carrot and bay leaf, and bring to the boil over a high heat. Remove any foam that comes to the top and reduce the heat to medium. Add the olive oil and salt, and simmer for about 20 minutes, or until the freekeh is just al dente. The timing may vary as there are different grades of grain.
2. Drain the freekeh and use tongs or a fork to remove the vegetables and bay leaf. Taste to see if you need to add a little more olive oil and salt. Best to do this when the freekeh is hot, as it will absorb the flavours better.
3. Transfer to a serving bowl and allow to cool before mixing in all the salad ingredients. Toss with a light hand to combine, and taste for seasoning again before serving.

Roasted spiced pumpkin with pickled apples

No other vegetable says autumn like pumpkin. Even if you set aside American traditions of carving and pies, the mere sight of a pumpkin evokes that autumn feeling, that long breath you take when the summer madness is over and you retreat indoors. We used to work in a catering kitchen set up in a converted chicken coop, in a little village on the outskirts of town. On our ride to work we would pass a big shed, which was empty all summer and then gradually filled up with pumpkins – the huge, wonky, slightly pale-skinned variety. As the season progressed, that shed filled with more and more of them. They looked like a funny community of misshapen heads. The days grew shorter and the shed became less and less crowded; the harvest was being dispatched to kitchens across the country to fulfil its delicious destiny: brightly coloured soups, sweetened stews, spiced purées. Cold weather food.

The pumpkin presents a particular problem to the home cook – what do you do with a vegetable that weighs as much as a small family member? Even if you're mad for it, like us, just one of them is still way more than one can handle.

We are lucky enough to live near a great greengrocer's run by a Portuguese family. They cut pumpkins into wedges so you only need buy as much as you want. Apparently, there are enough pumpkin lovers in our neighbourhood to get through a whole one without wasting any. If you can't buy just one wedge, do not despair – the little pumpkins you can get in most supermarkets now are great tasting and very handy: their flesh is tighter and smoother than that of big pumpkins, and you can often eat the skin as well, which saves on peeling.

If you're not quite ready for soups and stews, try this treatment: as a starter, a side or a light meal on its own, it features all the stars of the season – apple, bitter leaves, ginger, spice. And the tangy cheese just rounds it all off nicely.

A platter for a party or for 8–10 as part of a spread

For roasting

2 small Delica pumpkins or onion squash

1 tsp sea salt

½ tsp freshly ground black pepper

1 tsp sweet spice mix (see page 260)

2 tbsp baharat spice mix (see page 261)

2 pinches of chilli flakes

2 tbsp vegetable oil

1 orange (4 strips of the skin and all the juice)

60ml/4 tbsp water

For the dressing

1 Golden Delicious or Pink Lady apple

juice of 1 lemon

2 tbsp cider vinegar

a 5-cm/2-inch piece of fresh ginger

1 tsp honey

For the salad

1 small bag or large handful of washed baby spinach

1 head of red radicchio or endive, broken into leaves

100g/3½oz semi-hard goat's or sheep's cheese

1 tsp nigella seeds

1. Heat your oven to 220°C/200°C fan/425°F/gas mark 7.

2. Wash the pumpkins and use a scourer, if necessary, to remove any dirt or earth from the skins. Cut each one into eight wedges, remove the seeds and then cut each wedge in half across the middle (to create wide-based triangles). Place the pumpkin pieces in a flat roasting tin with the flesh facing upwards. Mix the salt and spices together in a small bowl. Drizzle the oil over the pumpkin and sprinkle with the spice mix – there is a lot of it and the spices should create a nice layer all over. Add the orange peel to the roasting tray. Place in the centre of the oven and roast for 10 minutes.

3. Remove from the oven, squeeze the juice from the orange all over the pumpkin and add the water to the tray. Baste a little, then return to the oven to bake for another 10–15 minutes or until a knife goes easily into the pumpkin flesh.

4. To make the dressing, finely dice the apple (with the skin on, for colour and texture) and place in a small bowl or jug. Add the lemon juice and vinegar, then peel the ginger and grate it into the apple. Add the honey and stir to combine.

5. Set the baby spinach and radicchio in an oven-proof serving dish or a large frying pan that can be placed in the oven. Top with the roasted pumpkin, and if any juice has accumulated in the bottom of the roasting tin, pour it over everything. Roughly crumble the cheese onto the pumpkin and sprinkle with the nigella seeds. Return to the oven for 5 minutes to melt the cheese a little before serving. If you want to prepare this stage in advance, the pumpkin keeps well for a few hours at room temperature; simply allow an extra 5 minutes to reheat when you are ready to serve.

6. As soon as the pumpkin comes out of the oven, douse it generously with the pickled apple dressing and serve straight away.

Red pepper, vine leaf and goat's cheese dolma cake

Those who are lucky enough to have a vine in their garden can enjoy the unique, green taste of fresh vine leaves. When very small, they can be torn into a simply dressed salad that epitomises the spring. Larger leaves can be wrapped around a mixture of rice and lamb and cooked slowly, the green flavour of the raw leaves changing into something a bit richer, with tones of resin and wood.

The rest of us can evoke those flavours by using vine leaves in brine (usually mature leaves cured in a salt solution). Their flavour is a different thing altogether. Richly savoury and slightly sour, they lend a magical tone to everything they are cooked with.

The traditional, best-known way to cook with vine leaves is to roll them into little cigars filled with seasoned rice and cook them slowly with lemon and oil – dolmades in Greek, yaprak in Arabic. A delicious but very time-consuming preparation, and one that requires dexterity and practice. Another, simpler, way to enjoy this lovely ingredient is to wrap it around small fish or pieces of meat, then grill or roast them. The brined leaves provide seasoning and flavour, and also protect the delicate flesh of, say, sardines or red mullet from drying out in the fierce heat, while still allowing them to take on that hint of smoke.

Here we offer another way – a bit of a centrepiece. It does require some work but it's nothing compared to the result, which, if we say so ourselves, is rather spectacular. Creamy goat's cheese and feta (seasoned with all manner of herbs, currants and roasted pine nuts) is encased in vine leaves – they complement each other so well. All this is wrapped again with roasted red peppers: silky-smooth, sweet and smoky, a bright red dress for this particular party girl.

Red pepper, vine leaf and goat's cheese dolma cake

A party piece for 8–10
or a main course for 6

6 large Romano red peppers

100g/3½oz drained vine leaves

For the filling

40g/1½oz/⅓ cup dried currants

40g/1½oz/⅓ cup roasted pine nuts

200g/7oz feta, crumbled

200g/7oz goat's cheese, crumbled

1 garlic clove, peeled and minced

10g/⅓oz chopped fresh mint (leaves from ½ small bunch)

10g/⅓oz chopped fresh parsley (leaves from ½ small bunch)

10g/⅓oz chopped dill (fronds from 1 small bunch)

1 tbsp chopped fresh thyme leaves or 1 tsp dried oregano

a pinch of freshly ground black pepper

2 tbsp cornflour

For the dressing

2 vine leaves, very finely chopped

15g/½oz/2 tbsp roasted pine nuts

1 lime, zest and then segment and cut into small dice

3 tbsp olive oil

1. Unless you have a BBQ in the back garden, set your grill at maximum heat and place the peppers under it for 10 minutes or until blackened on one side. Turn the peppers, using tongs, and grill for another 6–8 minutes till blackened all over. If you are using a BBQ or a gas burner, simply rotate the peppers over the flame until they are charred all over. Transfer to a large bowl or tray and cover with cling film, so they steam a little and cool.

2. While you are waiting for the peppers to cool, mix the filling ingredients together, but don't overwork the mixture. You can also mix the dressing ingredients together and set aside.

3. Once the peppers are cool enough to handle, peel off the skin and slit each one so that you can spread it out like a conical sheet of red cloth. Brush the seeds off, but don't worry if a couple stick around, and don't wash the peppers as you will lose so much of the great flavour.

4. Line a 23-cm/9-inch round baking tin with a sheet of baking paper, then line with the opened peppers, allowing lots of overhang. The best way is to place the tip of the pepper in the centre of the tin, and line the next one up with it, until you have covered the entire tin. Then repeat with the vine leaves. Put the filling in the tin, then fold the overhang back in to enclose it. You can make up to this stage in advance.

5. When you are ready to serve, heat your oven to 200°C/180°C fan/ 400°F/gas mark 6 and bake for 25 minutes. While you are waiting, mix all the dressing ingredients together, if you haven't already done so. Remove the cake from the oven and flip onto a serving platter. Top with the dressing and serve immediately with some crusty sourdough bread.

BBQ aubergine with jewelled rice salad

Anyone who spends time in the kitchen knows that there is no higher praise for a dish, no bigger compliment, than when someone likes it so much they want to know how it is made, in order to recreate it. There is a particular joy and sense of pride when someone cooks one of your recipes. We knew this even before we set out to write our cookbooks, but we are still surprised and moved to see pictures – whether on social media or by email – of other people preparing our favourite dishes at home, making them part of their repertoire, their lives and their shared memories with loved ones. It still feels like a very intimate form of communication; one we learn from all the time as our cooking and recipe-writing evolve and improve.

Of course, nobody owns a recipe. They are travellers, children of many parents, shape-shifters, always adapting to the place and time, taking the shape of the cook or culture, never twice the same. You are just a stop on a recipe's journey through time and other people.

That said, every cook has recipes that are harder to give away than others. Whether they are ones you worked on very hard or just stumbled upon by accident, these are the ones that really bring you the compliments, and that no one else makes. But the temptation to share also grows stronger, the better the dish is; and there is comfort and promise in the thought that, as you let go of one, another one will replace it – a better one, perhaps – like a strange food karma.

This tahini BBQ sauce is our little gem. It makes everything better. We use it to dress green beans and to roast lamb; it is great as a condiment and as a marinade; and a spoonful to finish a stew will give it immense richness and punch. I'm not sure of its origin, and the inclusion of soy sauce is decidedly not Middle Eastern, but when you're on to something this good, you don't ask questions, you just enjoy.

A firm favourite with our chefs and customers alike, this aubergine and jewelled rice salad really is the best thing you can do with this sauce – rich and creamy, spicy and sweet, it works so well with the aubergine flesh. The tangy rice salad makes this a very satisfying main course for vegans and meat-eaters alike.

So make this delicious sauce, make it your own, find great ways with it, and – please – if you enjoy it, drop us a line (we will be forever grateful) and, if you care to, please pass it on.

BBQ aubergine with jewelled rice salad

A party platter for 8–10 or a main course for 4–6

For the fragrant jasmine rice

250g/9oz/1⅓ cups jasmine rice (we favour Tilda)

1 tsp table salt

½ cinnamon stick

1 whole dried Persian lime, optional

1 tbsp vegetable oil

For the tahini BBQ sauce

1 garlic clove, peeled

4 spring onions (use the white parts and retain the green for the salad)

½ fresh green chilli, deseeded

250g/9oz/generous 1 cup tahini

2 tbsp soy sauce

1 tbsp red wine vinegar or sherry vinegar

4½ tsp date molasses, or you can use honey if you prefer

For the salad

1 butternut squash, peeled and cut in 2 x 2-cm/¾ x ¾-inch dice (about 600g/1lb 5 oz)

4–5 tbsp vegetable oil

3 aubergines, cut in half lengthways

4 spring onions (green parts only)

100g/3½oz dried cranberries

seeds from 1 pomegranate (retain some seeds to garnish)

1 small bunch of chives, chopped (retain some to garnish)

½ lime, very finely chopped (skin and all)

juice of ½ lime

sea salt and freshly ground black pepper, to taste

1. Bring 500ml/18fl oz/2 cups of water for the rice to the boil in a medium pan, then add the rice, salt, cinnamon, lime (if using) and oil, and bring back to the boil. Stir once or twice to loosen the rice, then reduce the temperature to the lowest setting and cover with a well-fitting lid. Allow to cook for 10 minutes, then turn off the heat. Leave covered for another 15 minutes before tipping the rice onto a large tray or plate to cool.

2. Roughly chop the garlic, white parts of the spring onions and chilli for the sauce, then whizz together in a food processor until puréed. Add the remaining sauce ingredients and 50ml/1¾fl oz/3½ tbsp of water and pulse until a thick paste has formed. Set aside.

3. Heat your oven to 240°C/220°C fan/475°F/gas mark 9. Place the butternut dice in a roasting pan or tray lined with some baking paper. Drizzle with two tablespoons of the vegetable oil, season with salt and pepper, and roast for 15–20 minutes until nice and golden.

4. Use a small knife to score the flesh of the aubergines in a criss-cross pattern, taking care not to cut through the skin. Cut each aubergine in half across the middle (widthways) and place on a roasting tray. Drizzle with the remaining vegetable oil and season with plenty of salt and pepper, then roast for about 20–25 minutes until golden.

5. Remove the aubergines from the oven and carefully spread a spoonful of the tahini BBQ sauce over the top of each. Return to the oven for 6 minutes to set as a light crust. (If you want to prepare the dish in advance, stop after roasting the aubergines to golden, and don't top with the tahini BBQ sauce or bake again until you are ready to serve.)

6. To assemble the salad, slice the green parts of the spring onions as finely as you can and stir into the rice. Add the roasted butternut dice, cranberries, pomegranate seeds, chives and finely chopped lime, and squeeze the lime juice all over. Mix very carefully to combine without mashing, and transfer to a serving platter or individual plates.

7. Top with the tahini BBQ aubergines and garnish with the chives and pomegranates you set aside earlier. If you wish, serve with some lime wedges on the side for added acidity.

Fish pastilla

Making a home-made pie is not a weekday undertaking for most of us, but instead is something for grand occasions. It is a true luxury, and a source of pride to the domestic cook who went to all the trouble: the filling, the pastry, the assembly, and finally the baking. The effort is evident and – when the result is good – much appreciated.

This one is a true party piece. Fiona, a dear friend of ours, was the first to try the recipe outside our kitchens and she served it on Christmas day. We have served it at the restaurant to many happy customers, a fair few of whom will be very pleased to see it here.

The preparation does have a few stages but nothing too complex – a mildly competent cook will get it all done without too much sweat – and there are some nifty little tricks along the way that boost the flavour without increasing the effort, like roasting the bass dry to get the flavour going, then adding water as it cooks. This not only keeps the fish nice and moist, it also creates a ready-made fish stock to use in the light, velvety sauce which beautifully binds the filling ingredients: the flaked flesh of the bass, small pieces of smoked haddock, and all the flavourings which bring a slightly north African accent to the dish. Tarragon is a good friend to all fish; bits of preserved lemon and pickled chillies or capers provide a tangy burst; and parsley keeps the whole thing fresh and sweet.

No one is expected to make filo pastry at home. Those of us who are pastry-phobic (or just can't be bothered) should always have a pack in the freezer. Wrap the filling with a few sheets, brush with butter to help it become irresistibly golden, and your work is done. Bring the whole pie to the table, piping hot. As you cut through it, the crisp shell will crack to reveal the creamy, succulent filling inside. You have toiled a bit in the kitchen; now enjoy your reward.

Fish pastilla

A party platter for 8–10
or main course for 4–6

To roast the fish

1 leek, slit in half lengthways

2 celery sticks

1 head of garlic, halved through
the middle to expose the cloves

½ lemon, quartered

1 large whole sea bass (1–1.2kg/
2lb 4–10oz), scaled and gutted

2 tbsp olive oil

1 tsp each whole coriander seeds,
fennel seeds and black peppercorns

1 tsp sea salt

For the filling

300g/10½oz smoked haddock (we
prefer the undyed type)

skin from 4 small preserved
lemons, chopped

6 pickled green chillies, chopped
(or you can use capers)

1 small bunch each of tarragon and
parsley, leaves picked and chopped

For the sauce

80g/2¾oz butter

1 leek, thinly sliced

80g/2¾oz/9⅔ tbsp plain flour

a generous pinch each of salt and
freshly ground black pepper

700ml/1¼ pints/3 cups drained
poaching liquid from the fish

To assemble

1 packet of filo pastry or
8 large sheets

60g/2¼oz melted butter

1. Heat your oven to 220°C/200°C fan/425°F/gas mark 7.

2. Place the leek, celery, garlic and lemon in a large, deep roasting tray. Make three or four large slits on each side of the fish, cutting through the skin. Place the fish on top of the vegetables, drizzle with the oil and sprinkle with the whole spices and salt. Roast in the centre of the oven for 15 minutes. Remove and pour 1 litre/1¾ pints/4⅓ cups of hot water carefully all over the fish. Return to the oven and bake for a further 10 minutes. Don't worry that the water isn't covering the entire fish; it is there to make a great stock.

3. Remove from the oven and allow to cool before gently lifting out the fish onto a clean tray. Strain the stock into a jug and set aside till later (you should have about 700–800ml/25–28fl oz/3–3½ cups). Carefully pull the skin off the fish, and flake the flesh off the bones and into a clean bowl. Don't worry if the fish breaks into little pieces; just take out all the bones. You can now discard the skin and bones.

4. Mix all the ingredients for the filling together in a large mixing bowl and add the flaked bass.

5. Melt the butter for the sauce in a small saucepan and add the sliced leek. Sauté a little until softened (about 1 minute), then add the flour all in one go and season with the salt and pepper. Stir well to combine, cook out for about 30 seconds, then gradually add the poaching liquid (topped up with water, if necessary) while stirring. Bring to the boil and let the sauce cook and thicken, stirring all the time. Once big bubbles appear, remove from the stove and cool a little before adding to the fish filling. Mix well. This can be prepared up to 24 hours in advance and left in the fridge until you are ready.

6. Spread the filo on your work surface. Brush the top sheet with the melted butter and lift it into a large oven-proof frying pan or casserole. Repeat with the remaining sheets, allowing lots to overhang the sides of the pan. If you are using small sheets, set them slightly off-centre each time to create the overhang around the edges. Fill with the fish filling and fold the overhang back in to enclose it. Let the filo settle in natural waves. Brush the top thoroughly with butter and bake at 220°C/200°C fan/425°F/gas mark 7 for 20–25 minutes until really golden all over.

7. Serve hot with a green leaf salad.

Chicken maklooba

To serve maklooba is not simply to serve a meal; it is to conduct a ceremony. A big pot is brought from the kitchen. The room fills with a gentle, savoury aroma, and great anticipation for a bit of drama. Strong arms, a quick, confident flick of the wrists, and the pot is flipped, bottom-up, onto a serving platter. The whole affair is ceremoniously laid on the table, all eyes now on the very proud cook. Traditions at this stage vary – some families take turns to tap the pot, others caress it gently, some just wave their hands above it like a blessing – but everyone takes part: family, friends, strangers. Everything else is put aside as the whole table is united in good wishes for the next stage of the show.

Higher drama this time. The second act: the pot is lifted gently, slowly, like curtains opening to reveal a stage. Scented steam rises from its contents. The big reveal and a moment of tension: will it keep its shape or collapse? If you are lucky and the shape holds, you will see a proud cake of saffron-gold rice with a colourful crown of bronzed vegetables on top, the different layers just visible from the side: tender meat, flecks of sweet onion. A world of goodness, a one-pot feast.

This is one of the best dishes of Palestinian cuisine, one that is served at family gatherings and on special occasions, a true showstopper that is surprisingly easy to prepare. The general idea is the same but, as is usually the case with these things, each family has its own variations: chicken, lamb or mutton can be used, offal if you like it, cauliflower, carrots, potatoes, courgettes, turnips – all are good candidates if you want to experiment. Traditionally the vegetables are deep-fried first, but we prefer roasting. Whatever you do, keep the spicing quite mellow – you don't want to overpower.

Now, I am an experienced chef and quite a big guy, but I am famously clumsy. The thought of turning a heavy, hot pan onto a plate, and doing it while people were watching, made me quite nervous. It shouldn't have. It's a very simple exercise, but if you are serious about your cooking (and if you are still reading this, I suspect you are) it may not be a bad idea to practise the flip with an empty pot when no one is watching.

Some years ago, I had the good fortune of joining a feast at the table of a patrician Arab family in east Jerusalem. The pot was brought in and turned by the matron of the house; she must have done it hundreds of times before. We all tapped on it together, the pot was lifted, the cake collapsed a bit, we all gasped and laughed. A sprinkle of pine nuts and fresh parsley, we each got our portion, and then went back for more. It was an incredibly delicious meal, yes, but it's the whole theatre, the way we all got involved, which turned a great meal into a truly magical experience.

A party platter for 8–10
or a main course for 4–6

4 carrots, peeled and cut into
1-cm/⅜-inch slices
(about 250g/9oz)

3 courgettes, washed and cut into
2-cm/¾-inch slices
(about 500g/1lb 2oz)

2 potatoes, peeled and cut into
2-cm/¾-inch slices
(about 500g/1lb 2oz)

1 small cauliflower, broken into
small florets (about 500g/1lb 2oz)

4–5 tbsp olive oil

8 skin-on chicken thighs (I prefer
to keep them on the bone)

4 long banana shallots (or 2 small
red onions), peeled and sliced

1 cinnamon stick

320g/11¼oz/1¾ cups
basmati rice

a generous pinch of saffron

1 tsp salt

½ tsp freshly ground black pepper

750ml/1⅓ pints/3¼ cups boiling
water

1. Heat your oven to 220°C/200°C fan/425°F/gas mark 7 and line a large roasting tray with baking paper. Place the vegetables on the tray, drizzle with the olive oil and season with a little salt and pepper. Roast for about 20 minutes until nicely golden.

2. Place a very large pot on a medium heat and put the chicken thighs, skin-side down, in one layer – all eight thighs should fit. Season the exposed side of the thighs with some salt and pepper. Allow the skin to crisp and colour, but not burn. This process takes time, about 15–20 minutes. Fat will start to seep out of the thighs and you can check the colour occasionally but don't be tempted to flip them until the skin is beautifully golden. Once they are ready, flip the thighs and cook for 5 minutes on the other side, then remove from the pot to a plate, leaving the fat rendered from under the skin in the pot on the heat. Add the shallot slices and cinnamon stick to the fat and stir-fry for 3–4 minutes. Once the shallots have softened, add the rice, saffron, salt and pepper and mix to coat. Tip the rice mixture into a bowl.

3. Now assemble the dish: sprinkle three large tablespoons of the rice mixture over the base of the pot, and place all the roasted vegetables on top. Cover with half of the remaining rice, then arrange the chicken pieces on top. Pour over any juices that have accumulated on the plate, and then top with the rest of the rice. Place the pot on a high heat and give it 2 minutes to warm up. Pour over all the boiling water (carefully as it will sizzle up). Allow to come to the boil then reduce the heat to minimum. Cover with a well-fitting lid or a sheet of aluminium foil. Leave to cook for 35 minutes, then carefully remove the lid and check if there is still any visible water – use a spoon to push the rice aside a little to check. If you can still see some liquid, cover and cook for another 10 minutes, but if there is no water visible, remove from the heat, cover and allow to rest for 20 minutes before serving.

4. When you come to serve, remove the lid and place a large serving platter on top of the pot. Holding the plate firmly, flip the pot upside-down onto it. Let it settle a bit, then tap the pot – or get everyone to do it – and gently lift to reveal the maklooba. We like serving this with tahini, fresh parsley leaves, roasted pine nuts and some lemon wedges. There are some, who cut a circle of baking paper and line the base of the pot to make sure everything comes out in one go. You can try it, if you wish, but then where is the fun? The flavour is great, even if the maklooba doesn't come out whole.

Lamb chops with rocket, figs and walnuts

It is almost an axiom in cooking that lamb chops should be pink. It's a really nice way to cook them, for sure, but it's equally nice sometimes to cook them all the way, giving them a deep mahogany outside, which crisps up deliciously. Do not ask your butcher to trim the chops. What is called 'French trim' is the biggest kitchen folly and waste – removing the tastiest, sweetest meat just to get a clean bone for presentation is idiocy in my book. The whole joy of lamb chops is eating them with your fingers and picking at them until there is no more meat on the bone. Try cooking them this way; you may never go back to pink.

A party platter for 8–10 or a main course for 4–6

2 untrimmed racks of lamb, separated into single chops

For the salt rub

½ tsp table salt

½ tsp freshly ground black pepper

½ tsp ground cumin

½ tsp ground fennel seeds

For the salad

1 small bag rocket, washed

4–6 fresh figs (depending on size), quartered

50g/1¾oz/⅓ cup walnuts

2 large shallots, peeled and sliced

6 sage leaves

a pinch of salt

a pinch of sugar

3 tbsp red wine or sherry vinegar

1. Mix the ingredients for the salt rub in a small bowl. Season the chops on both sides with all the salt rub, then stack them one on top of another in two piles to recreate the two lamb racks. Set a heavy skillet or heavy-based frying pan on a medium-low heat. Place one of the stacks of chops as one in the frying pan, fat-side down, and cook for about 10 minutes, allowing the skin to crisp and the fat to render. Drain the fat into a bowl, transfer the chops to a plate, then repeat the process with the second stack.
2. While this is happening, place the rocket on a large serving plate and add the fig quarters.
3. When the skin on the lamb has crisped, break the stacks up and place as many chops flat in the pan as you can fit in one layer (you will have to do this in a few batches, as there won't be enough room to lay them all flat in the pan at once). You can add a little of the fat you drained off earlier, if needed. Also, if you have a BBQ, it is great to finish these on it, for added smokiness. Increase the heat and allow to colour for 2 minutes, then flip and colour the other side. Remove the chops to your serving plate, laying them on top of the rocket, and repeat until all the chops have been seared.
4. Add the walnuts, shallots and sage leaves to the same pan you used for the lamb, and fry for a minute or two, stirring and scraping to get all the tasty bits from the bottom of the pan. Season with the pinch of salt and sugar, then add the vinegar and remove from the heat. Spoon all over the salad and lamb chops, and serve.

Royal mansaf

In the Hashemite kingdom of Jordan there is no party or gathering without this dish. Here it gets the royal treatment with a gilding of no small amount of saffron. This dish comes back to our menu every year around Christmas time, when something truly festive is in order. This is a complex preparation that requires serious kitchen time and commitment, so ensure that whenever you make it, it will count.

This is a long recipe with many stages. We thought about not including it, but so many of our guests and customers have asked for a version, so here goes. In order to make life easier, you can split the preparation over a couple of days. Cook the lamb, shred it and strain the liquids on the day before you want to serve this, and store in the fridge until needed. You can make the carrot base for the rice in advance and pop that in the fridge too. The following day, prepare the rice and the sauce. Then you just need to heat the lamb and put everything together.

A party platter for 10–12 or a main course for 6–8

To slow-cook the lamb

1 onion, quartered

1 garlic head, halved

1 orange, halved

1 lamb shoulder

2 tsp salt

½ tsp white pepper

2 dried Persian limes, halved or cracked

2 cinnamon sticks

1 tbsp coriander seeds

1 tbsp fennel seeds

½ tsp ground turmeric

1.4–1.5 litres/2½–2¾ pints/ 6–6½ cups boiling water

1. Heat your oven to 250°C/230°C fan/500°F/gas mark 9. Place the onion, garlic and orange in a large, deep roasting tin or heavy-based casserole. Lay the lamb shoulder on top, season all over with the salt and pepper and roast for 20 minutes. Remove from the oven and sprinkle over all the spices apart from the ground turmeric. Return to the oven for 5 minutes, then reduce the temperature to 220°C/200°C fan/425°F/ gas mark 7. Mix the turmeric with the boiling water and add to the tin. The liquid should reach about halfway up the shoulder, so use the amount you need to suit your pan.
2. Cover and return to the oven for another 30 minutes. Remove from the oven, baste well, reduce the temperature to 200°C/180°C fan/400°F/ gas mark 6, re-cover and cook for 1 hour.
3. Remove from the oven, uncover and carefully turn the shoulder upside-down. Baste well, return to the oven, reduce the temperature to 180°C/160°C fan/350°F/gas mark 4 and roast for another hour.
4. Repeat the basting and flipping process and cook for a further hour. Then baste once more and cook until the lamb pulls away easily from the bone – the full cooking time will depend on many factors, so this last stage may take anything from 30 to 60 minutes. You can serve the lamb now, if you like, without the pilaf.

For the saffron rice pilaf

4–5 tbsp fat from roasting the lamb (or use olive oil)

2 onions, peeled and very finely chopped

4 carrots, peeled and coarsely grated

1 orange, halved

1 cinnamon stick

a pinch of saffron

500g/1lb 2oz/2¾ cups basmati rice

½ tsp salt

a pinch of cayenne pepper

750ml/1⅓ pints/3¼ cups stock (the remaining lamb cooking liquid topped up with water as necessary)

For the yogurt sauce

250ml/8¾fl oz/generous 1 cup of the cooking liquid

a pinch of saffron

300g/10½oz/1⅓ cups yogurt

1 egg yolk

1 tbsp cornflour

To garnish

120g/4¼oz/1½ cups flaked almonds, toasted

150g/5¼oz/1 cup golden raisins, soaked in boiling water

1 small bunch of parsley, leaves picked and chopped

5. If you are making the full recipe, leave the lamb to cool in the cooking liquid for a couple of hours. Fat will rise to the surface; skim off four or five tablespoons of it and set this aside for making the carrot base. Carefully lift the lamb onto a platter. Strain the remaining cooking liquid – you should have about 600–700ml/21–25fl oz/2½–3 cups of stock. Set aside 250ml/8¾fl oz/1 cup for the yogurt sauce, and retain the rest for cooking the rice.

6. Shred the lamb off the bone in large chunks, discarding any sinew or big lumps of fat. Drizzle two or three tablespoons of the cooking liquid over the lamb. Cover and either place in the (turned-off) oven to keep warm until your rice is ready, or (if you are splitting preparation over two days) keep in the fridge until needed. Once you are ready with the rice and sauce the next day, you can pop the lamb in the oven at 200°C/180°C fan/400°F/gas mark 6 for 15 minutes, or you can use a microwave to heat through.

7. Heat the fat for the rice in a large saucepan on a medium setting. Add the onions, carrots, orange halves, cinnamon stick and saffron, and cook for about 10 minutes, stirring occasionally. Reduce the heat to low and continue cooking really slowly for an hour, stirring every now and then. It needs to reduce and concentrate the flavours, so allow it to cook down, and even start to stick to the base of the pan.

8. Now add the rice, salt and cayenne. Stir well to combine and increase the heat to high so that the rice can really heat through. Add all the stock at once and bring to the boil. Cover, reduce the heat to low and cook for 10 minutes. Remove from the stove and keep covered for a further 10 minutes while you make the sauce.

9. Heat the cooking liquid for the sauce in a small saucepan and add the saffron. Mix the yogurt with the egg yolk and cornflour, then slowly whisk into the hot cooking liquid. Stir till it thickens and just comes to the boil. Remove from the heat and set aside until you are ready to serve.

10. Top the rice with the lamb (remember to warm it up if you have stored it in the fridge), then drizzle with all the sauce and sprinkle with the flaked almonds, golden raisins and chopped parsley.

Tahini cake with lemon and white chocolate

We are recipe-hunters. Our flat is filled with bits of paper scribbled with rudimentary instructions from friendly cooks we meet on the way; pages we've torn from newspapers and foreign magazines with a picture we like and a recipe we will one day translate; menus with cryptic notes written after drunken dinners (what did we eat that made us write 'coriander before and after, also lamb, must try', and what does it mean?). Our phones are also filled with pictures, not only of dishes we liked but also of recipes we will one day try, in our never-ending search for lovely things to cook, serve and eat.

Most of these recipes never get made, but every so often, when we have some headspace and free time, we go through these papers, take recipes to the kitchen and try them. Most will be made once and never be revisited, even if the results were good, because that is not the point of the exercise: whenever you follow a recipe, you follow in someone's footsteps, getting a glimpse of their mind and their experience, and there is always something interesting to take from that. But then sometimes, rarely, we come across a recipe that is so good, so special, and so right for us, that we return to it again and again, and it becomes part of our experience, our minds.

This is one such recipe, found in a drawer in our kitchen, torn from a newspaper – neither of us remembers which one, but it has an American feel because it uses buttermilk and peanut butter. Whoever wrote the recipe said tahini could be used instead, which was all the encouragement we needed. A seemingly simple sponge, not much to look at, but the taste and texture of it are so special, so good – nutty, fudgy, sweet with a savoury touch – that we (and everyone who tried it) fell instantly in love. We added white chocolate and lemon zest to the original recipe, and vanilla cream for show. We bake it almost every day now and know it'll be part of the Honey & Co cake repertoire for years to come, and now hopefully yours too.

Tahini cake with lemon and white chocolate

Makes a two-tier 23-cm/9-inch round cake fit for kings, and a large party

For the cake batter

320g/11¼oz/1¾ cups caster sugar

350g/12⅓oz/2⅔ cups plain flour

1½ tsp bicarbonate of soda

1½ tsp baking powder

1 tsp table salt

zest of 2 lemons

70g/2½oz white chocolate, chopped

2 eggs

120ml/4¼fl oz/½ cup vegetable oil

230g/8¼oz/1 cup tahini paste

seeds of 1 vanilla pod or 1 tbsp pure vanilla essence

240ml/8½fl oz/1 cup buttermilk or kefir

For the icing

250g/9oz/generous 1 cup mascarpone

200g/7oz/scant 1 cup double cream

200g/7oz/scant 1 cup full fat plain cream cheese

90g/3¼oz/⅔ cup icing sugar

1 tbsp vanilla essence or 1 pod

2 tbsp rum

For sprinkling (optional)

30g/1oz/¼ cup chopped white chocolate

a sprinkling of lemon zest

1. Heat your oven to 190°C/170°C fan/375°F/gas mark 5.
2. Mix all the dry ingredients for the cake batter together in a large bowl. In a smaller one, mix the eggs with the oil, tahini, vanilla and buttermilk. Pour the egg mixture into the dry ingredients and stir to combine. Slowly stir in 180ml/6¼fl oz/¾ cup boiling water, and mix until well incorporated.
3. Line the base of two 23-cm/9-inch round cake tins with a circle of baking paper and lightly butter the sides. Divide the batter evenly between the two tins and bake in the centre of the oven for 15 minutes. Rotate the tins for an even bake, then cook for another 10–15 minutes. The cakes should feel lovely and bouncy, and have a good, golden colour all over. Remove from the oven and carefully flip onto a flat plate to flatten the tops. Allow to cool upside-down before removing from the tins.
4. Mix all the icing ingredients together with a small whisk until well combined and thickened (you can pop this in an electric mixer, but best to use a paddle attachment to avoid overworking and splitting it). Place the first cake on the serving platter, spoon on half the icing, and spread around to cover. Top with the second cake, spoon on the rest of the icing, and spread. If you wish, sprinkle with chopped white chocolate and lemon zest.
5. If serving on the same day as baking, best to avoid putting the cake in the fridge. If you are keeping it for longer, do place it in the fridge but allow to come to room temperature before serving.

Cherry pistachio Bakewell

This recipe contains some great ingredients: pistachios and cherries are two of our favourite things. It also contains a small amount of spinach. Shocking, but it really works. You can hardly taste it, but – as in carrot cake – the vegetable keeps the baked filling moist, to produce frangipane like you've never tried before. The bright green colour is a wonderful bonus too. A different way of getting your kids to eat their greens.

To fill a long rectangular tart tin or a 20-cm/8-inch round pie tin (best to use a loose-based tin)

For the pastry

100g/3½oz soft butter, diced

50g/1¾oz/¼ cup caster sugar

120g/4¼oz/¾ cup + 2½ tbsp plain flour

40g/1½oz/4¾ tbsp wholemeal flour (or use more plain flour)

40g/1½oz/⅓ cup finely ground pistachios (blitz in a food processor)

1 egg, lightly beaten

For the cherry filling

30g/1oz/2½ tbsp caster sugar

300g/10½oz/2 cups fresh cherries, pitted

For the pistachio cream

100g/3½oz/¾ cup zshelled pistachios

100g/3½oz soft butter

90g/3¼oz/½ cup caster sugar

1 whole egg

1 egg yolk

a pinch of salt

20g/3/4oz/2⅓ tbsp plain flour

20g/¾oz wilted spinach

For the garnish (optional)

20g/¾oz/3 tbsp shelled pistachios, roughly chopped

1. Place all the ingredients for the pastry together in a mixer with a paddle attachment and mix until the dough comes together to a ball. Remove and wrap in cling film. Place in the fridge and leave to rest for at least 30 minutes before rolling out thinly and lining your tin. Place in the fridge until all the other components are ready (the pastry doesn't need to be pre-baked).

2. Heat a frying pan on a high setting and sprinkle in all the sugar for the cherry filling. Stir until it starts to melt and caramelise, then add the cherries. Continue to stir until all the sugar has dissolved. Keep the heat high and cook for 5 minutes, then reduce the heat to very low and continue cooking for another 5 minutes until you have a very thick compôte. Set aside to cool a little. Heat your oven to 190°C/170°C fan/375°F/gas mark 5.

3. Put the pistachios for the cream in a food processor and blitz to a powder, then add the butter and sugar and blitz again. Finally add the whole egg, yolk, salt, flour and cooked spinach and blitz everything to a homogenous green paste.

4. Spread the cherry compôte over the base of the pastry shell, top with the green pistachio paste (I use a piping bag for an even topping, but you can use a spoon or spatula), and sprinkle with the roughly chopped pistachios, if using.

5. Place in the centre of the oven for 15 minutes, then carefully rotate the tray for an even bake and leave for a further 15 minutes, or until set and lightly greenish-gold. The filling should feel rather firm. Allow to cool in the tin before removing and serving.

Chocolate pecan slice with oranges

The gym is the church of our times, it seems; the great unifier. Everybody goes: the elderly, the prepubescents, the career mums, and the hipsters who look like they rolled out of bed; every creed and colour. I only found this out recently. I hate exercising and, having spent my adult life in hot kitchens, I felt as if I had had my fair share of sweating, and so there was no need for me to do any more of it in my precious time off.

We chefs, like athletes, tend to plump up as we age. When you are young and starting out in the profession, the hard physical work keeps you trim and fit. You burn more calories in a shift than most people do in their whole working day, and then some. You can eat whatever you want and it doesn't show. Things change when you reach your mid-thirties. Your job becomes less gruelling, more managerial. You are faced with a choice: eat less or work out more. Eating less has never really been an option for me, so I joined the gym, and joined society.

My local recreation centre in Brixton is a testament to the power of good architecture and design. A brutalist masterpiece, it is vast and generous; it has a climbing wall, courts for tennis and squash, a gym with a window to the swimming pool, a swimming pool with a window to the town centre. Everything you could possibly need if you want to exercise, or – more accurately in my case – really don't want to exercise, but feel that you must. It is such a good facility that it's probably the one place where Brixton, an area of extreme and varied demographics, really comes together. Representatives from the African, Jamaican and Portuguese communities, affluent newcomers, the kids from the council block around the corner, and at least one tubby Israeli chef running and cycling nowhere – all of us side by side.

A lovely young couple had lunch at our restaurant. Healthy-looking and happy, they enjoyed their food. They debated sharing one dessert between them, but decided to have one each: what the hell, another hour at the gym tomorrow, they said. But with a warning – it'd better be worth it! I went to ask them later if it was; they were happy. They come to us often now, and never skip pudding.

If you are like the rest of us, toiling away at the gym, sweating off your supper, it's a good idea to make sure that when you do indulge, it is really worth it. This one really is, especially if you like chocolate (how can one not?). A crunchy pecan base, and the chocolate on top is creamy and rich but not at all cloying; it is quite good enough on its own but becomes truly special if you add the toppings – and why wouldn't you? You worked for it.

Note: this dessert is suitable for people on a gluten-free diet, and for those who don't work out. It is a very rich slice and will be enough for 8 people, but also keeps well in the fridge. You don't have to make all the garnishes, it is delicious just as it is, but if you want to make it a real show stopper, give it a try.

Chocolate pecan slice with oranges

Makes 1 large loaf (our tin is 30 x 10cm/11¾ x 4 inches, but something similar will do)

For the base

150g/5¼oz/1¼ cups pecans, finely chopped (we prefer to chop by hand to obtain a very rough crumb, but you can use a food processor)

½ tsp sea salt

zest of 1 lemon

1 egg

For the chocolate filling

100g/3½oz 70% cocoa dark chocolate

60g/2¼oz slightly salted butter

40g/1½oz/generous ½ cup date molasses, or you can use dark honey

3 medium eggs

150g/5¼oz/¾ cup dark brown sugar

zest of 1 orange

For candied orange strips (optional)

strips of peel from 1 orange

5 tbsp sugar

For the candied pecans (optional)

50g/1¾oz/scant ½ cup pecan halves

2 tbsp sugar

For the orange segments (optional)

segments from the 2 oranges you used for zest and peel strips

1. Heat your oven to 190°C/170°C fan/375°F/gas mark 5. Line the base and sides of your tin with a single large strip of baking paper. Mix the base ingredients together, tip into the tin, and press down to flatten and cover the bottom completely. Bake for 12 minutes.

2. In the meantime, melt the chocolate with the butter and molasses in the microwave or over a double boiler. Lightly whisk the eggs with the sugar and orange zest – just enough to combine well, but not aerate. Stir the melted chocolate into the egg mixture until well-combined, then pour over the part-baked base. Return the tin to the oven and cook for a further 20–24 minutes. The filling will still be soft, but should have changed to a nice opaque chocolate colour on top, rather like a brownie. Allow to cool a little then place in the fridge to set for at least a couple of hours, or overnight, before removing from the tin.

3. To assemble, remove the chocolate pecan slice from the fridge, take it out of the tin and peel off the baking paper (it should all peel off easily). Place on a serving plate, top with your choice of fresh orange segments, candied pecans and candied orange strips, if using, and serve.

Optional extras for the top

For the candied orange strips, cut the orange peel into long, thin strips. Place in a small pan, add enough water to cover, bring to the boil, then drain. Repeat this twice. Put the boiled, drained strips back in the pan, add 150ml/5¼fl oz/scant ⅔ cup of water and the sugar, and bring back to the boil. Reduce the heat to minimum and simmer for 6 minutes. Remove from the heat and allow the orange strips to cool in the syrup.

For the candied pecans, place the pecans in a frying pan and heat lightly for 1–2 minutes, stirring the nuts around all the time. Sprinkle with the sugar and continue stirring as the sugar coats the nuts all over and starts to melt. When it starts to darken, quickly pour the nuts onto a sheet of greaseproof paper and, using two spoons, separate them from each other. Leave to form lovely, individual, crispy shells as they cool.

For a crowd

Marunchinos

The Sephardi community of Jerusalem really know what to do with almonds. They make the best marzipan using the traditional method, adding almond paste to boiling sugar syrup at just the right moment. They also make these biscuits when there is something to celebrate. The lightest crunch on the outside gives way to a wonderfully chewy centre. The dried apricots are not traditional, just glorious.

Makes 16

250g/9oz/2½ cups ground almonds

250g/9oz/1¾ cups icing sugar, plus about 150g/5¼oz/1 cup icing sugar to coat

zest of ½ lemon

1 heaped tbsp orange blossom honey

90g/3¼oz egg white (about 3 eggs' worth)

70g/2½oz/½ cup dried apricots, diced in small cubes

2 tsp orange blossom water

1. Line a baking tray with baking paper. Place the ground almonds and icing sugar in a large bowl and mix together. Add all the remaining ingredients (except the icing sugar for coating) and mix to a smooth, fluffy, wet kind of dough. Cover and place in the fridge to set for about 30–60 minutes.

2. Divide into 16 pieces, each about 40g/1½oz. Shape into balls and roll in the additional icing sugar. You can leave them as balls, but for a festive traditional look, pinch each one between the thumb and forefinger on both hands to create a star-like shape.

3. Set aside to dry and form a bit of a crust. Anything between one hour and two will do.

4. Heat the oven to 200°C/180°C fan/400°F/gas mark 6. Bake on the lined tray for 8 minutes, then rotate the tray and bake for a further 2–3 minutes until very lightly golden. Cool on the tray and store in an airtight container at room temperature.

Peanut and cocoa nib brittle

150g/5¼oz/generous 1 cup raw peanuts, peeled

350g/12⅓oz/1¾ cups sugar

70g/2½oz butter

60g/2¼oz/scant ½ cup raw cocoa nibs

1 tsp flaky sea salt

1. Heat your oven to 190°C/170°C fan/375°F/gas mark 5. Line a large flat tray, preferably one with a little rim, with baking paper or a silicone sheet. Place the peanuts on the tray and roast in the centre of the oven for 8 minutes.

2. In the meantime, put a heavy-based frying pan or large saucepan on a high heat and sprinkle two tablespoons of the sugar over the base. As soon as it starts melting, add another two tablespoons and reduce the heat to medium to allow more control. Use a wooden spoon to stir the sugar until just melted, then repeat with another two tablespoons again and again until all the sugar is in the pan. Continue stirring until it starts to turn a lovely golden caramel colour. Don't let it go too far, as it will continue cooking when you add the butter, but make sure it is all dissolved.

3. Remove from the heat, add the butter in one go and mix well to combine. It will sizzle up, then split a little and become darker. Continue stirring till all the butter is incorporated and you have a smooth, rich caramel. Add the still-warm peanuts along with the cocoa nibs and salt, and mix well to coat thoroughly. Quickly transfer to the warm tray you used for roasting the peanuts and spread the mixture out a little. If it starts to set in a thick clump, you can pop it in the oven for 5–6 minutes to smooth it out a little.

4. Leave to cool entirely on the tray. Don't be tempted to touch it until it is cold. Then break it into shards and store in an airtight container or cookie bags.

Pistachio, cardamom and rose marzipan

Makes about 20

160g/5¾oz/1⅔ cups ground pistachios (use a food processor or a spice grinder)

130g/4½oz/¾ cup + 2 tbsp icing sugar

zest of 1 lemon

½ tsp ground cardamom

1 tsp rose water

juice of ½ lemon (you may only need a splash or two)

1. Mix all the marzipan ingredients together using as much lemon juice as needed to combine to a smooth dough. Work it by hand to help the oils come out of the nuts to create the perfect paste.

2. Tear off pieces of about 15g/½oz each and roll into balls. You can roll these in chopped pistachios or rose petals or both, or you can shape them any other way you prefer.

Donkey

We called him 'Donkey' affectionately: he was hard-working but clumsy, a bit thick but always content, and never angry. His real name was Adriano and he didn't look like a donkey at all. In fact he was exceptionally beautiful, with sparkling green eyes and a goofy smile, and muscles from all his hard work in the kitchen and hours in the gym. He knew it too; he could never concentrate when there was a mirror around, mesmerised by his own beautiful reflection. An eighteen-year-old farm boy from Brazil, he came to London and started washing dishes in the Ottolenghi deli and café on Ledbury Road. He was working sixteen-hour days, and at one point was even sleeping in the kitchen on a pile of dirty laundry under the stairs in order to save on rent until Yotam, the owner, came one night and found out. He wasn't fired; Yotam put him up in his spare bedroom for a couple of months.

By the time we joined Ottolenghi, Adriano had already been promoted to prep chef, and – like everyone else who met him – we fell in love. Because he was funny and fun; because he was clumsy and stupid, and charming about it; because no matter what, he was always by our side, pushing with us. He would stay back with us on Friday night till all the Saturday prep was done, and he was there on Saturday morning when you couldn't keep up with the orders. He was there when the fridge needed cleaning and the bathroom was blocked, or when you had thousands of canapés to make for a wedding. And even though he was a terrible cook, even though he was prone to the most ridiculous accidents, and even though he would sometimes do things so stupid the mind would boggle, whenever he was there, things were more fun.

We worked together shoulder-to-shoulder, day after day, for over three years. We saw people come and go, meet and get married. We would gossip and laugh, go out to eat, diss each other's wardrobe and friends and skills, get in and out of trouble. When I went to a new job in the company, he was with me. When Sarit headed a big project, there he was with her, like a good luck charm, a mascot. I'm not sure when he started calling me 'Papa' and Sarit 'Mami', or when we stopped calling him 'Donkey' and started calling him 'Baby'.

Beautiful, stupid Adriano turned out to be smarter than all of us. All the money he made from years of hard work, all the rent saved by sleeping on the floor, all of it went to buy land in Brazil. A lot of it. His brother and father planted guava and peaches, tending them for him. We would get daily updates on the state of his farm: the tractor he was going to buy, the weather, the price of guavas at different times of the year, endless pictures of trees. By the age of twenty-eight he was a rich landowner. He didn't need to do our prep anymore, he needed to go back and, in a very literal sense, enjoy the fruits of his labours.

We went on to open Honey & Co. We had not stayed in touch but I always knew he would come back one day, flaunting his success and flashing his guava cash, while we would still be in the kitchen on a Friday night, prepping aubergines for the next day

Saturday night service in Honey & Smoke, and everything went wrong: the early tables arrived late, the late tables arrived early, everyone wanted to eat at the same time, and we were pressed. At 7pm two of the floor staff left the shift (one in tears, one in anger), and at 9pm, when every table was full, the fire alarm started wailing for no apparent reason and would not stop for the longest ten minutes of my life. In the world of restaurants, nights like this are not uncommon and I'm an old restaurant hand, but still, I left that night quite shaken up. Checking my phone on the way to the tube there was a message – there'd been an accident, Adriano had died. A dumb Brazilian prank I thought, but it wasn't. There was an accident; there were pictures. You should see the tractor. Actually, you really shouldn't. He was only 32.

Somewhere in Brazil there was a funeral, heartbroken parents and siblings, and many friends, I'm sure. There were guavas and peaches to pick, box and sell. Here in London we were choking on our tears. We had nowhere to put our sorrow. All the next day the phones pinged at us – people we haven't heard from for ages, all the old crew coming out of the woodwork: the crabby old pastry chef calling from Japan, another one from France. We were too far apart to come together in one place for a wake, but we reached out for each other, really needing to talk about a clumsy, beautiful boy who loved money and sex and church and his own reflection in the mirror. We told each other all the stories we knew already, like how every time he would go upstairs to grab some vegetables we would hear a crash, and then see lemons rolling down the stairs, followed by a tumbling Adriano. Like the time the porter banged his head and Adriano tried to help him by applying burn cream. Like the time Colleen sent him to get Christmas cards and he came back with a stack of Mother's Day cards instead because they were on sale. Like how he nearly got us all put in jail. And Cornelia talked about her first day at work, when she saw him for the first time, and said, like she always does when she tells this story: 'He was the most beautiful boy I have ever seen…'.

Sorrow comes, unannounced and unwanted. Love always brings the risk of pain with it. Big life events – the happy ones, the sad ones – require a ritual, a way for us to be with each other and share what's really important: our sadness, our joy or regret, our gratitude or hope, and a bite to eat.

For the kitchen

In a parallel universe, there is a couple similar to us. They live in a little village amongst beautiful fields, not far from a Mediterranean shore. They have a small but very functional kitchen with a beautifully stocked larder, filled with tomatoes and fruit they preserved in the summer, beans and pulses and mountain herbs that they dried themselves, jars of pickles, home-made cheese, and beautiful spice mixes blended by them. In that kitchen, there is always time to spare, and there are always the makings of a good meal for whoever's around. There is always a cake, and some bread fresh out of the oven, something bubbling on the stove, and plenty of cookies and biscuits, the baking of which has been perfected through years of trial and error.

The fresh produce that comes into that kitchen is superb: eggs from the chickens, which are picking in the yard under the fruit trees and tomato plants, fish from the nearby shore, only the best of the season. Everything in that kitchen is carefully selected with beauty and function in mind – from the pots, pans, knives and chopping boards to the cookbooks that line the shelves.

This is the alternative existence of our fantasies, fuelled, most likely, by reading too many cookbooks and not taking enough holidays. We usually revert to it at the end of an especially hard day or week. When work is unrelenting and nothing seems to go our way, when London seems unforgiving and hostile, when we come home to our disorganised kitchen that never seems to have anything useful or beautiful in it, we think about this couple, who could have been us, in their little house, and wish we were them.

To live out our fantasies, at least in part, we have opened a little deli across the road from Honey & Co. We carefully stock its shelves with jars of the jam we make; bags of the cookies we bake; excellent spices, nuts, grains and pulses; the finest tahini, olive oil, honey and syrups we can find; delicious wine from all over the world; fresh fruit and vegetables in their prime; really good pots and pans; lovely glasses; our favourite cookbooks. We bake fresh bread every day – two types. There are dips and pickles in little pots, ice cream we churn, and a lot of cake. For lunch, we lay a counter full of fresh salads, pies, stews and roasts. It's the dream kitchen, and much more.

We are old enough now to know that we live the life that suits us. We could never be that fantasy couple: we love our hectic life just as it is. We love London – its pace and the parks and the weirdos; we love our flat with its wonky floors and our cluttered kitchen; we love our 16-hour days in the restaurant kitchens, and the daily dramas that come without fail. And, deep in our hearts, we feel sorry for that other couple in their little house in the middle of nowhere, shelling beans and canning tomatoes, bored out of their minds.

Sweet spice mix

We use this mostly for cakes and baked goods, and also for savoury preparations that require a lighter touch. Most importantly, it is the base for the savoury spice mix, giving it an extra layer of flavour.

10 cardamom pods
6 cloves
½ nutmeg
1 tsp whole fennel seeds
2 tsp whole mahleb seeds
3 tsp ground ginger
4 tsp ground cinnamon

1. Heat your oven to 190°C/170°C fan/375°F/gas mark 5. Roast the cardamom pods, cloves and nutmeg on a baking tray for 5 minutes, then add the fennel and mahleb seeds and roast for another 5 minutes. Remove from the oven and allow to cool completely before grinding to a fine powder.
2. Mix with the pre-ground ginger and cinnamon, and store in a dry, airtight container. This will keep for up to six months, but I always think you should try to use it within two months to get the flavour at its best.

Baharat spice mix

This is our version of baharat or Lebanese mixed spice. You can use ready-made baharat or Lebanese seven-spice mix, which can be found in supermarkets, but they will give a slightly different flavour to the end result, so make your own if you want to recreate the Honey & Co flavour at home. Our spice mixes are the essence of our cooking.

1 dried chilli

3 tsp coriander seeds

4 tsp cumin seeds

2 tsp ground pimento/allspice

1 tsp ground white pepper

½ tsp ground turmeric

2 tsp sweet spice mix (see opposite)

1. Heat your oven to 190°C/170°C fan/375°F/gas mark 5. Crack the dried chilli open and shake out the seeds.
2. Place the deseeded chilli on a baking tray with the coriander and cumin seeds, and roast for 6 minutes. Remove from the oven and allow to cool completely on the tray.
3. Crumble the chilli between your fingers, then grind to a powder with the other roasted spices. Mix with the dried ground spices and store in a dry, airtight container. It will keep for up to six months, but ideally use within two months for the full effect.

262   For the kitchen

Ras el hanout spice mix

There are as many versions of this spice mix as there are spice shops in the Middle East. The literal translation of ras el hanout is 'head of the shop', meaning the best the shop has to offer. It can contain up to twenty different spices and can be bought ready-made, although if you make it freshly yourself, you will taste the difference.

60g/2¼oz/½ cup cumin seeds

60g/2¼oz/¾ cup coriander seeds

90g/3¼oz/1 cup fenugreek seeds

3 whole cloves

2 dried Persian limes

30g/1oz/3¾ cups whole cardamom pods

20g/¾oz dried rose petals

20g/¾oz curry leaves

1 tsp cayenne pepper

1 tbsp ground white pepper

1 tbsp ground turmeric

1 tbsp ground cinnamon

1 tbsp amchoor (mango powder)

1 tbsp sweet paprika

1. Heat your oven to 190°C/170°C fan/375°F/gas mark 5. Place the cumin, coriander, fenugreek, cloves, dried limes and cardamom pods on a baking tray. Roast for 5 minutes, then add the rose petals and curry leaves to the tray and roast for another 3 minutes.

2. Remove from the oven and cool before using a spice grinder to grind them to a powder. Mix with the pre-ground spices and store in a dry, airtight container. It will keep for up to six months, but ideally use within two months for the full effect.

For the kitchen

Amba spice mix

Making amba spice mix may require a trip to a good spice vendor (or a special order online) to purchase the Persian limes and the amchoor powder, which may be a bit of a faff, but it is the only way to try these amazing flavours without leaving this country. This mix is usually used to make amba relish or sauce (see below and page 266) but it can also be used in other preparations to add a tang and an extra kick. Roasting pumpkins or sweet potatoes with a sprinkle of amba spice, or adding it to meatballs or fish kofta, is a great idea.

100g/3½oz/generous 1 cup fenugreek seeds

50g/1¾oz/7 tbsp ground turmeric

3 dried Persian limes

50g/1¾oz/5½ tbsp yellow mustard seeds

1 tsp cayenne pepper

50g/1¾oz/½ cup amchoor (mango powder)

1. Use a spice grinder or a little coffee grinder to blitz all the spices together (no need to roast any of them).
2. Mix well to combine and store in a dry, airtight container. This will keep for up to six months, but ideally use within two months for the full effect.

Amba sauce

The origins of amba sauce most likely lie in India. It was brought to Israel by the Iraqi Jewish community in the middle of the twentieth century, and it is now a daily staple in Israel's street food, where it gets drizzled or scooped all over shawarma and falafel – a combination you should try. It is usually made of fermented sour mangoes and fenugreek. We use sweet mangoes because the sour ones are not generally available here. The result is slightly different, but sensationally good.

This recipe and the following one are our take on traditional mango sauce and the chunkier relish-like condiment that comes in jars. Both go well with roasted chicken and lamb, and roasted vegetables like cauliflower and aubergine. They also work a treat with an Indian takeaway. Both taste best if you wait a day after making them before serving, and will keep well for about a week in the fridge.

100ml/3½fl oz/scant ½ cup vegetable oil

2 tbsp amba spice mix (see page 265)

flesh from 1 mango, blitzed to a purée

juice from ½ lemon

½ tsp salt

1. Slowly cook the oil and spice mix in a saucepan on a medium heat until very fragrant and a little bubbly. Add the mango purée and whisk till combined, then bring back to the boil.
2. Stir in the lemon juice and salt, then remove from the heat and cool. Transfer to an airtight container or a jar, and keep in the fridge. It will last for up to two weeks.

Amba relish

2 mangoes (best to use slightly underripe ones)

2 tsp salt

50ml/1¾fl oz/3½ tbsp vegetable oil

1 tbsp amba spice mix (see page 265)

2 tsp ground fenugreek

a pinch of cayenne pepper

juice of 1 lemon

1. Peel the mango, cut off the cheeks and dice them into nice small cubes. Place the dice in a sealable container and sprinkle with one of the teaspoons of salt. Seal and leave overnight in a cool room (if you are in the middle of summer, the fridge might be better).
2. Use all the rest of the mango flesh, including any trimmings, to make a purée. You should end up with about same volume of dice and purée. Keep the purée refrigerated till you cook it.
3. The next day, warm the oil over a low heat for a few seconds, then add the spices and the second teaspoon of salt. Stir to toast until the spices start to foam a little, about 30–40 seconds. Add the mango purée, mix till combined well, then increase the heat to medium and bring to the boil. Stir well, making sure not to let it stick or burn, then fold in the cubed mango and lemon juice. Continue stirring till the chutney boils again, then remove from the heat and cool. Transfer to an airtight container or a jar, and keep in the fridge. It will last for up to two weeks.

Courgette pickle

This is a quick pickle: it is ready within a few hours and is best eaten within 3–4 days of making. As this pickle doesn't keep well for long, it is not one for preserving summer, but rather one to make when you have a glut of courgettes.

For the salting

4 courgettes, trimmed and sliced into 1-cm/⅜-inch rounds

1 tsp table salt

For the pickling liquid

50g/1¾oz/¼ cup caster sugar

200ml/7fl oz/scant 1 cup cider vinegar

1 tsp ground turmeric

1 tsp mustard seeds

1 tsp whole fennel seeds

2 bay leaves

1 garlic clove, peeled and sliced

a few sprigs of tarragon or ½ tsp dried tarragon

1. Place the slices of courgette in a sieve resting over a bowl and sprinkle with the salt. Mix together a little, then leave to drain for at least 30 minutes, and up to an hour, so that some of the liquid in the courgettes is released.
2. Heat 150ml/5¼fl oz/scant ⅔ cup of water for the pickling liquid with the sugar to dissolve it (or simply pour the same amount of boiling water from a kettle onto the sugar). Then add all the other ingredients and mix well.
3. Transfer the courgettes to a container and pour over the liquid. Cover and let everything steep together in the fridge for a couple of hours, then they are ready to serve. The pickles will get stronger with every day that passes, and will only keep for up to four days.

Quince pickle

2 quinces

80g/2¾oz/6½ tbsp sugar

200ml/7fl oz/scant 1 cup rice wine vinegar

1 cinnamon stick

1 dried chilli

This is an excellent accompaniment for roasted rich meats such as duck, goose or game, or as part of a cheese platter.

1. Cut the quinces into quarters, leaving the skin on, then use a peeler to shave off thin layers so that each slice has a sliver of skin, which will help them keep their shape.
2. Place the quince slivers in a saucepan and cover with the sugar, vinegar and 100ml/3½fl oz/scant ½ cup of water. Add the cinnamon stick and chilli, then place on a low heat and cook for about 30 minutes until the slivers turn a deep pink and are very soft. Transfer to an airtight container, allow to cool, and store in the fridge. This will keep well for about two weeks.

Kohlrabi pickle

For the salting (start a day in advance)

2 whole kohlrabi

2 tsp salt

For the pickling liquid

100ml/3½fl oz/scant ½ cup white wine vinegar

1 tsp mustard seeds

2 bay leaves

1 tsp amba spice mix (see page 265)

1. You will need to sterilise a large jar before you begin. To do this, heat the oven to 200°C/180°C fan/400°F/gas mark 6 and wash the jar (and its lid) in hot soapy water. Rinse well and dry thoroughly with a clean tea towel. Place on a baking tray and heat in the oven for 5 minutes. Alternatively pour boiling water into the clean jar, count to ten, then pour the water out and fill the jar immediately with your pickle ingredients.
2. Peel the kohlrabi and cut into even-sized dice. Place in the sterilised jar, sprinkle with the salt, close and set aside overnight at room temperature. If you like your pickles funky, you can leave it for another night – just shake it about a little after the first night to mix the salt around.
3. Mix all the pickling liquid ingredients together (no need to heat them) with 150ml/5¼fl oz/scant ⅔ cup of water, then pour over the kohlrabi in the jar to cover completely. Leave the jar on a windowsill for two days before moving to the fridge, where the pickles will last well for up to a month. These are best eaten cold.

Red pepper pickle

A special thank you to our dear friend Couscousul for telling us about these pickles that his mom makes. His description of them sent us running to the kitchen in an attempt to re-create them. We are not sure how they compare to the originals – we've never tried them – but these pickles certainly get lots of compliments from our guests.

4 red peppers

2 bay leaves

1 tsp coriander seeds

1 tsp whole black peppercorns

1 whole dried chilli

1 tsp fennel seeds

2 garlic cloves, peeled and sliced

1 tbsp salt

80g/2¾oz/6½ tbsp sugar

200ml/7fl oz/scant 1 cup cider vinegar

1. Halve the peppers, remove the seeds, cut into thin slices and place in a large bowl. Add the bay leaves, coriander seeds, peppercorns, chilli, fennel seeds, garlic and salt and stir well to combine.
2. Heat 200ml/7fl oz/scant 1 cup of water with the sugar and vinegar and bring to the boil. Pour over the peppers and mix well. Transfer to an airtight container or a jar, seal and leave to cool.
3. Transfer to the fridge once cooled. They will be ready to eat the following day, and will keep well for a couple of weeks.

Red cabbage pickle

**For the salting
(start two days in advance)**

1 red cabbage, halved, cored and thinly sliced

1 tbsp salt

For the pickling liquid

200ml/7fl oz/scant 1 cup white wine vinegar

1 tsp salt

1 tbsp dark brown sugar

2 whole pimento/allspice berries

2 bay leaves

2 dried chillies

½ tsp whole black peppercorns

1. You will need to sterilise a large jar before you begin. To do this, heat the oven to 200°C/180°C fan/400°F/gas mark 6 and wash the jar (and its lid) in hot soapy water. Rinse well and dry thoroughly with a clean tea towel. Place on a baking tray and heat in the oven for 5 minutes. Alternatively pour boiling water into the clean jar, count to ten, then pour the water out and fill the jar immediately with your pickle ingredients.
2. Mix the thin slices of cabbage with the salt and push them into the jar so they are tightly packed.
3. Seal the jar and leave at room temperature overnight. The next day, shake the jar well, open it to let out air, then seal again and leave at room temperature for another night.
4. The following day, boil all the ingredients for the pickling liquid together with 400ml/14fl oz/1¾ cups of water and pour over the cabbage. Seal and leave to rest at room temperature for one more day before transferring to the fridge to store. This will keep well for a month.

For the kitchen

Green tahini

1 small bunch of parsley,
leaves only (no stalks)

1 small garlic clove, peeled

½ tsp amba spice mix
(see page 265)

½ tsp ground fenugreek

1 tsp salt

juice of 1 lemon

300g/10½oz/1⅓ cup
tahini paste

1. Place everything except the tahini paste in a food processor (or use a hand-held stick blender) with 300ml/10½fl oz/1¼ cups of cold water and blitz together until the mixture resembles a green milkshake.
2. Add the tahini and blitz again until you get a smooth paste. Taste, and adjust the seasoning if needed. This will keep for up to four days in the fridge, but you may need to refresh it with a splash of lemon juice or water, as it will get thicker and thicker.

Chermoula paste

This versatile paste lends itself to a multitude of dishes, from rice cooked with prawns to quick chicken hotpot, or even spread on a toasted cheese sandwich. It will keep well for a week in the fridge and can even be frozen for future use.

2 preserved lemons, skin only
(pulp removed)

10 garlic cloves, peeled

1 red chilli, trimmed
but seeds left in

1 bunch of coriander,
top leafy part only

1 bunch of parsley, leaves picked

2 tbsp ground cumin

1 tbsp smoked paprika

1 tsp ground ginger

1½ tsp acı biber salçası (Turkish
pepper paste) or tomato purée

about 50ml/1¾fl oz/3½ tbsp olive
oil

1. Blitz the lemons, garlic and chilli to a rough pulp in a food processor. Add the herbs, spices and pepper paste and blitz till smooth.
2. Remove to a small bowl and add just enough olive oil to bind to a paste. Store in the fridge until you are ready to use.

Shata

This is a simple preparation – the chillies are salted, blitzed to a pulp and left to ferment – but it develops a beautifully complex flavour. It will gladly lend itself to whatever you mix it with, and is a great addition to vegetable dishes or stews that need a bit of a kick. If you buy more chillies than you need, do prepare this, even if you're only making a tiny bit – it'll go a long way.

500g/1lb 2oz red chillies

4 tbsp salt

50ml/1¾fl oz/3½ tbsp olive oil

1. Cut the chillies into thick rings (we leave the seeds in) and push them into a jar. Sprinkle with the salt, screw on the lid and shake well. Leave on the windowsill for about a week, shaking the jar every day. The chillies should release a lot of liquid and become rather limp.

2. After a week, open the jar carefully and drain the chillies. Use a food processor (and a mask to protect your nose and mouth) and purée them to a rough pulp.

3. You will need to sterilise a large jar for the next stage. To do this, heat the oven to 200°C/180°C fan/400°F/gas mark 6 and wash the jar (and its lid) in hot soapy water. Rinse well and dry thoroughly with a clean tea towel. Place on a baking tray and heat in the oven for 5 minutes. Alternatively pour boiling water into the clean jar, count to ten, then pour the water out and fill the jar immediately.

4. Transfer the chilli purée to the sterilised jar, cover the top with a finger-depth layer of olive oil (about 1½cm/⅝ inch), and leave to rest for another week at room temperature before using. Once opened, store in the fridge. It will last well over a month, but you may develop an addiction before that.

Pilpelchuma

This North African trick is somewhere between a spice mix and a paste. It makes a good base for sauces – just add water – or can be used to great effect as a rub for roasting meat, or on strong-flavoured fish like bream or mackerel on the grill.

4 tbsp minced garlic (about 1 head, peeled and minced)

3 tbsp olive oil

4 tbsp sweet paprika

4 tbsp smoked paprika

2 tsp caraway seeds, roughly ground

2 tsp cumin seeds, roughly ground

4 tbsp tomato purée

4 tbsp acı biber salçası (Turkish pepper paste) or double the tomato purée

4 tbsp lemon juice

2 tsp sugar

1. Fry the garlic in the olive oil till fragrant. Add the spices and fry for 1 minute, then add the tomato purée, pepper paste, lemon juice and sugar. Stir and cook out till it is well combined and starts to boil a little.
2. Remove to an airtight container and store in the fridge. It will last well for a couple of weeks.

Zehug coriander relish

1 large bunch of coriander (about 40g/1½oz), top leafy part only, washed well

1 green chilli

1 small plum tomato

1 garlic clove, peeled

½ tsp salt

3 tbsp olive oil, plus more to seal

1. Finely chop the coriander, chilli, tomato and garlic. Mix together with the salt, then transfer to a little bowl. Add the olive oil and combine to make a paste.
2. Transfer to an airtight container, drizzle over a little more oil to create a seal so the zehug doesn't discolour, then store in the fridge for up to one week. Or you can freeze it in small amounts in an ice cube tray, and pull out a cube at a time.

Sweet zehug

1 bunch of coriander, top leafy
part only, washed well

1 small bunch of parsley,
leaves picked

1 garlic clove, peeled

1 large green chilli, trimmed but
with seeds left in

a pinch of salt

1 tbsp honey

½ tsp ground cardamom

40ml/8 tsp olive oil,
plus more to seal

1. Blitz all the ingredients, apart from the olive oil, to a rough paste in a
food processor, then transfer to a small bowl. Stir the olive oil through,
taste and adjust the seasoning as necessary.

2. Transfer to an airtight container, drizzle over a little more oil to create
a seal so the zehug doesn't discolour, then store in the fridge for up to
one week. Or you can freeze it in small amounts in an ice cube tray, and
pull out a cube at a time.

Basic instructions (the way we work)

In recipes where it matters, I have stated the end (net) weight of prepared vegetables and fruits to give you a better idea of size. In most of our recipes, however, there is no need to get too hung up on the weights, which are there as guidance.

I do most of my baking and roasting in a fan-assisted oven, as it is faster and has better heat distribution than a conventional oven. However, ovens vary greatly and I have tried to give other indications as to the end result you are looking for. In most cases you should use your discretion as regards your own oven and how it affects cooking times.

We use a lot of nuts in our food, and the recipe will always state whether they should be roasted or not. If you are roasting them, the best way is to lay them on a baking tray in the centre of the oven at the temperature and for about the time set out on page 279. They should go a light golden colour or, in the case of pistachios, greeny-golden. Don't let them brown unless the recipe requires it, as they will become bitter, and do remember that they will continue to roast on the hot tray even after you remove it from the oven, so if you think you left them in a little too long, quickly transfer them to a cold bowl to stop them cooking any further. You can also roast nuts on the hob in a dry frying pan on a very low heat, shaking the pan every few seconds. This requires more attention, but far less electricity, than oven-roasting. Don't roast more than you need (apart from the ones you intend nibbling on) as the flavour is best when freshly roasted.

We always use fresh garlic and not pre-minced, as the flavour changes when it has been sat around for too long.

We use freshly squeezed lemon juice for the same reason.

When we say sugar, we mean granulated sugar unless otherwise specified, and salt means table salt unless otherwise stated. We use Maldon sea salt to finish dishes, rather than to cook with, unless the recipe specifically calls for sea salt as an ingredient.

We try to grind our own spices wherever possible, the only exceptions being ground turmeric, ginger, pimento/allspice berries and cinnamon, which are all hard to grind on your own. We love using a small coffee grinder, but a pestle and mortar is really good too (and makes you feel that you've worked for your flavour). Avoid buying pre-ground spices if you can, or make sure to buy from a shop with a high turnover so that they are really fresh.

We use quite a lot of cinnamon sticks in our cooking. They are interchangeable with cassia bark, which I actually prefer as it imparts a mild hint rather than a strong hit. If you are using very thick, tightly rolled cinnamon quills, use half the amount in the recipe. Don't replace with ground cinnamon.

Chilli is an issue for us. I am not a huge fan. I like a tiny note of spice that brings out the flavour. Itamar loves spicy, hot food, and enjoys the sensation of little beads of sweat forming on his nose when he eats. The amounts given in the recipes are my preferences. I recommend you start with these, as you can always add more, but it is harder to reduce the chilli-hit once it is in. The heat will also greatly depend on the season and the type of chilli. In general terms, the larger the chilli, the milder it is; and in summer I find that they get an extra kick from the sun and are spicier. Removing the seeds and white membrane reduces the heat if you want to take it down a notch. The best way to decide how much to use is to cut a tiny piece off the end of the chilli and taste it: if it kicks you in the mouth, take it easy.

Please read the entire recipe before you start cooking, or indeed shopping. It is always good practice.

A few notes on ingredients

We have tried not to use too many strange or hard-to-come-by ingredients in this book, as it is all about the comfort and ease of home-cooking, however a few things have crept in that you may not use on a daily basis. It is easy to find them all on the internet now, and even we have an online webstore at www.honeyandco.co.uk where you can buy what you need for this book (and our previous ones too).

In case you have any concerns about buying something for one recipe and never using it again, we have set out below a few words about some of our favourite 'unusual' ingredients, along with the recipes in which we have used them, plus some additional hints and tips, so that you can justify the purchase. We probably don't need to say this, but please don't get too hung up on finding all the right ingredients – if you can't find something (or can't be bothered to), just wing it. It'll be fine.

Tahini

Buying tahini for this type of cuisine is not an option – it's a necessity. There are very few preparations that aren't improved with a little tahini.

We strongly favour Lebanese, Israeli or Palestinian light-coloured, smooth tahini, and we never use Greek or health-store-style whole/dark tahini (made with unhulled sesame seeds) as they are not to our taste.

Tahini paste keeps well at room temperature. You should shake the jar vigorously before using to distribute the fat and solids evenly.

Always use cold water when making raw tahini paste into a dip. Use a 50:50 paste-to-water ratio to get the best results for your base, i.e. 300g/10½oz paste to 300ml/10½fl oz cold water. Traditionally all you need to add for a great dip is lemon juice, garlic and salt, but mixing in herbs, tomatoes, peppers and spices in addition works well too.

40   Lamb stew with medjool dates (and sometimes tahini)
45   Arayes
86   Fried cauliflower, amba and tahini
90–1   Lentil stew with burnt aubergine, eggs, tahini and zehug
98   Yemeni lentil meatballs
145–46 M'sabaha
181–82 Frozen tahini parfait and chocolate sandwich-cake
221–22 BBQ aubergine with jewelled rice salad
228–29 Chicken maklooba
239–40 Tahini cake with lemon and white chocolate
272   Green tahini

Dates and date molasses

Dates are among the oldest and simplest sweeteners in the world, and using the syrup extracted from them is a great natural way to add sweetness and depth.

You can use date molasses (a.k.a. date honey) as a replacement for golden syrup, honey and even maple syrup; of course this will result in a slightly different flavour to the finished dish, but it will always be delicious. It's not just for cooking with either: try it on a slice of bread with a smothering of tahini paste, or simply drizzle over your yoghurt and fruit.

40   Lamb stew with medjool dates (and sometimes tahini)
156   Medjool date, honey and macadamia breakfast loaf
181–82   Frozen tahini parfait and chocolate sandwich-cake
221–22   BBQ aubergine with jewelled rice salad
245–46   Chocolate pecan slice with oranges

Orange blossom water and rose water

Flower waters are mostly used in desserts, but they can also impart great aroma to a salad dressing, giving it a little something special. Another excellent use is to add floral notes to a jug of iced tea. Orange blossom water and rose water can easily be omitted from a recipe without too much effect, but for that extra layer of flavour, it is worth buying a bottle of each. You will soon find yourself using them in trifles, steamed puddings and cocktails.

Use in moderation, and make sure you are buying a flower water and not an oil, as the latter can be too potent to cook with.

82   Roasted carrots with pistachio cream, coriander seeds and honey
84   Fennel, kohlrabi, orange and chilli salad
248   Marunchinos
114   Lemon and saffron posset
184   Frozen meringue bar with strawberry and lime
252   Pistachio, cardamom and rose marzipan

Harissa

Harissa paste is now (thankfully) a common condiment in London supermarkets, and is (hopefully) spreading around the country. It is a great chilli paste that isn't too spicy but gives your food a real kick. Make sure you buy one in which the chillies are preserved in oil, and ideally with the addition of rose for aroma and flavour. If you can only find the harissa paste that comes in small, squeezy tubes, use it with care as it is much spicier than the one we recommend. You can use harissa paste whenever a dish calls for chilli, and it works well when used as a marinade for roasting meat and fish too.

42   Tinned tuna cakes
67   Zaalouk
142   Harissa and lemon chicken sandwich
143   Tuna, capers and roasted pepper sandwich
201   Pumpkin chirshi
204   Harissa and goat's cheese buns

Saffron

Buying good saffron is expensive – it is a hugely labour-intensive crop to harvest – but it is worth it, and it will last a while. Use in moderation so as not to overpower (a pinch is about 6-8 strands, not more). It will impart plenty of flavour, so don't be cheap. Invest and enjoy.

26   Saffron carrot soup with a little bit of rice
49   Essaouira fish tagine
50   Prawn, pea and potato tagine
78–9   Pear and saffron salad with walnut tahini
111–12   Feather blade braised with pumpkin, spices and prunes
114   Lemon and saffron posset
228–29   Chicken maklooba
234–35   Royal mansaf

Turkish pepper paste – acı biber salçası

This is a great paste made with sundried chilli peppers. It isn't as easy to obtain as some of the other ingredients on this list, although you can find it online in a few places. Equally, if you are traveling to Turkey, or just going to a Turkish grocer's, definitely buy a jar. You can use it in pasta sauces and tomato-based dishes, and as a marinade for roasting meat.

200   Kamunia – a different kind of chopped liver
272   Chermoula paste
274   Pilpelchuma

Spice mixes

We make four essential spice mixes ourselves: sweet, savoury (baharat), ras al hanut and amba. They are worth the effort of making and storing, I promise. And even if you end up making them without one or two of the spices we use, they will still be far better (and fresher) than store-bought versions.

If you really can't be bothered, you should be able to find good baharat spice and ras al hanut easily enough in a large supermarket. The sweet spice mix is a harder one to buy in this country, as is amba spice, but if you find yourself in a market in the Middle East, seek out some to take home with you.

Chilli flakes

We use dried chilli flakes in many of our recipes. We favour the lighter, citrusy tang and spice of Turkish biber chilli flakes or Aleppo chilli flakes (the latter is sadly becoming harder to come by, because of the political situation in Syria), but many types exist. Some are much spicier, while others can be rather bitter, so it is worth trying a tiny pinch before using them – that way, you can judge for yourself how much you want to add.

Allspice a.k.a. pimento

This berry (sold whole or ground) has an extremely complex flavour – it tastes like a combination of cinnamon, black pepper, nutmeg and mace, all rolled into one. If you can't find any allspice/pimento, use a pinch of each of the above instead.

Roasting nuts

Type of nut	Oven temperature	Length of time
Whole almonds, skin on	180°C/160°C fan/350°F/gas mark 4 (nice and low, to roast without burning)	14–15 minutes
Flaked almonds	190°C/170°C fan/375°F/gas mark 5	6–8 minutes
Pine nuts	200°C/180°C fan/400°F/gas mark 6	5 minutes, shake the tray and roast for another 5–8 minutes until golden
Pistachios	190°C/170°C fan/375°F/gas mark 5	8–10 minutes
Walnuts	190°C/170°C fan/375°F/gas mark 5	10 minutes
Hazelnuts	180°C/160°C fan/350°F/gas mark 4 (nice and low, to roast without burning)	14–16 minutes

Index

A

almonds: marunchinos 248
amba: amba relish 266
  amba sauce 266
  amba spice mix 265
  fried cauliflower, amba and tahini
    sauce 86
apples, roasted spiced pumpkin with
  pickled 214–15
apricots: marunchinos 248
  roasted duck legs with clementines and
    apricots 106
arak: fennel crackers with arak and
  sugar 202
arayes 45
artichokes: baked artichokes with
  lemony ricotta dip 73–4
aubergines: BBQ aubergine with
  jewelled rice salad 221–2
  burning aubergines 64–5
  lentil stew with burnt aubergine, eggs,
    tahini and zehug 90–1
  Romanian white aubergine dip 69
  silky green aubergine purée 69
  stuffed aubergine boats 100
  Turkish yogurt bread with aubergine
    filling 133–34
  zaalouk 67

B

Baharat spice mix 261
Bakewell, cherry pistachio 242
BBQ aubergine with jewelled rice salad
  221–22
beans: borlotti beans on toast with soft-
  boiled eggs 28–9
beef: arayes 45
  celeriac mafrum 152–53
  feather blade braised with pumpkin,
    spices and prunes 111–12
  hedgehog meatballs 38
  shishbarak 149–50
  spring lamb meatballs with broad
    beans and courgettes 95–6
  steak fatoush salad with grapes and
    tomatoes 31
  Yemeni lentil meatballs 98
biscuits: marunchinos 248
  sumac and vanilla shortbread 56
  see also cookies
black currants, chocolate cloud cake
  with red and 117
borlotti beans on toast with soft-boiled
  eggs 28–9

bread: arayes 45
  borlotti beans on toast with soft-boiled
    eggs 28–9
  crispy pitta shards 172
  fig and feta pide 128–29
  harissa and lemon chicken sandwich
    142
  Jerusalem sesame bread 137–39
  roasted tomato and manouri cheese
    sandwich 143
  sardines with roasted tomatoes and
    crispy pitta 177–78
  tuna, capers and roasted pepper
    sandwich 143
  Turkish yogurt bread with aubergine
    filling 133–34
brittle, peanut and cocoa nib 250
broad beans: spring lamb meatballs with
  broad beans and courgettes 95–6
broccoli: brown wheat and broccoli
  salad with sesame dressing 89
  tuna dip with broccoli, potato and
    eggs 70
buns, harissa and goat's cheese 204
butter, pepper and chilli 108–9
butternut squash: spiced butternut
  squash phylas 209

C

cabbage pickle, red 270
cakes: chocolate cloud cake with red and
  black currants 117
  chocolate financiers with coffee cream
    120
  frozen tahini parfait and chocolate
    sandwich cake 181–82
  marmalade and dried fruit cake 160
  medjool date, honey and macadamia
    breakfast loaf 156
  pear and walnut upside-down cake
    163–64
  pistachio and cranberry cake 161
  rich fruit cakes 158–61
  strawberry ricotta cakes 118
  tahini cake with lemon and white
    chocolate 239–40
cannellini bean hummus 108–9
capers: tuna, capers and roasted pepper
  sandwich 143
cardamom: pistachio, cardamom and
  rose marzipan 252
carrots: roasted carrots with pistachio
  cream, coriander seeds and honey
  82

saffron carrot soup with a little bit of
  rice 26
cauliflower: fried cauliflower, amba and
  tahini sauce 86
celeriac mafrum 152–53
cheese *see* feta; goat's cheese; manouri;
  ricotta
chermoula paste 272
  Essaouira fish tagine 49
cherries: cherry, herb and freekeh tabule
  212
  cherry pistachio Bakewell 242
chicken: chicken braised in spicy
  matbucha and cracked wheat pilaf
  103–4
  chicken in plums and sweet spice 33–4
  chicken maklooba 228–29
  harissa and lemon chicken sandwich
    142
chicken livers: kamunia 200
chickpeas: harira soup 20–1
  m'sabaha 145–46
  roasted Romano peppers, chickpeas,
    olives, roasted tomatoes and cumin
    210
chillies: fennel, kohlrabi, orange and
  chilli salad 84
  pepper and chilli butter 108–9
  shata 273
chirshi, pumpkin 201
chocolate: chocolate cloud cake with red
  and black currants 117
  chocolate financiers with coffee cream
    120
  chocolate pecan slice with oranges
    245–46
  frozen tahini parfait and chocolate
    sandwich cake 181–82
  milk chocolate chip cookies with
    coffee beans 53
  peanut and cocoa nib brittle 250
  tahini cake with lemon and white
    chocolate 239–40
  white chocolate chip, currant and
    orange cookies 54
chorizo: harira soup 20–1
clementines: roasted duck legs with
  clementines and apricots 106
cocoa nibs: peanut and cocoa nib brittle
  250
coconut and lime pancakes with mango
  52
coffee: chocolate financiers with coffee
  cream 120

milk chocolate chip cookies with coffee beans 53
cookies: honey and spice cookies 154
milk chocolate chip cookies with coffee beans 53
white chocolate chip, currant and orange cookies 54
coriander: roasted carrots with pistachio cream, coriander seeds and honey 82
zehug coriander relish 274
courgettes: chicken maklooba 228–29
courgette pickle 267
spring lamb meatballs with broad beans and courgettes 95–6
cracked wheat pilaf 103–4
crackers: fennel crackers with arak and sugar 202
cranberries: pistachio and cranberry cake 161
cream: coffee cream 120
pistachio cream 82
currants: shishbarak 149–50
white chocolate chip, currant and orange cookies 54
custard fruit tart, baked 186

D
dates: lamb stew with medjool dates 40
medjool date, honey and macadamia breakfast loaf 156
dips: lemony ricotta dip 73–4
pumpkin chirshi 201
Romanian white aubergine dip 69
taramosalata 198
tuna dip with broccoli, potato and eggs 70
dolma cake, red pepper, vine leaf and goat's cheese 217–18
doughnuts, smoked haddock 195–96
dressing, sesame 89
dried fruit: marmalade and dried fruit cake 160
pistachio and cranberry cake 161
rich fruit cakes 158–61
duck: roasted duck legs with clementines and apricots 106
dumplings: shishbarak 149–50

E
eggs: borlotti beans on toast with soft-boiled eggs 28–9
green shakshuka 23–4
lentil stew with burnt aubergine, eggs,

tahini and zehug 90–1
mushroom scrambled eggs 27
spinach, egg and filo pie 93
tuna dip with broccoli, potato and eggs 70
Essaouira fish tagine 49

F
fatoush salad: steak fatoush salad with grapes and tomatoes 31
fennel: fennel crackers with arak and sugar 202
fennel, kohlrabi, orange and chilli salad 84
feta: fig and feta pide 128–29
Israeli couscous with tomatoes, feta and lemon 36–7
potato and feta fritters 19
red pepper, vine leaf and goat's cheese dolma cake 217–18
stuffed aubergine boats 100
figs: fig and feta pide 128–29
fig relish 76
lamb chops with rocket, figs and walnuts 232
filo pastry: fish pastilla 225–26
spiced butternut squash phylas 209
spinach, egg and filo pie 93
financiers, chocolate 120
fish: Essaouira fish tagine 49
fish pastilla 225–26
sardines with roasted tomatoes and crispy pitta 177–8
smoked haddock doughnuts 195–96
tinned tuna cakes 42
tuna, capers and roasted pepper sandwich 143
tuna dip with broccoli, potato and eggs 70
fish roe: taramosalata 198
freekeh: cherry, herb and freekeh tabule 212
fritters, potato and feta 19
fruit: baked custard fruit tart 186
see also dried fruit
fruit cakes 158–61
marmalade and dried fruit cake 160
pistachio and cranberry cake 161

G
garlic: borlotti beans on toast with soft-boiled eggs 28–9
chermoula paste 272
pilpelchuma 274

garlic leaves: silky green aubergine purée 69
goat's cheese: baked goat's cheese wrapped in walnut pastry with fig relish 76
harissa and goat's cheese buns 204
red pepper, vine leaf and goat's cheese dolma cake 217–18
roasted spiced pumpkin with pickled apples 214–15
grapes: steak fatoush salad with grapes and tomatoes 31
green shakshuka 23–4
green tahini 272

H
haddock: smoked haddock doughnuts 195–96
harira soup 20–1
harissa: harissa and goat's cheese buns 204
harissa and lemon chicken sandwich 142
hedgehog meatballs 38
herbs: chermoula paste 272
cherry, herb and freekeh tabule 212
honey and spice cookies 154
hummus, cannellini bean 108–9

I
Israeli couscous with tomatoes, feta and lemon 36–7

J
Jerusalem sesame bread 137–39

K
kamunia 200
kohlrabi: fennel, kohlrabi, orange and chilli salad 84
kohlrabi pickle 268

L
lamb: lamb chops with rocket, figs and walnuts 232
lamb stew with medjool dates (and sometimes tahini) 40
lamb tagine with runner beans and tomatoes 48
royal mansaf 234–35
spring lamb meatballs with broad beans and courgettes 95–6
stuffed aubergine boats 100
Yemeni lentil meatballs 98

leeks: green shakshuka 23–4
  hedgehog meatballs 38
  mushroom scrambled eggs 27
lemons: harissa and lemon chicken
    sandwich 142
  Israeli couscous with tomatoes, feta
    and lemon 36–7
  lemon and saffron posset 114
  lemony ricotta dip 73–4
  tahini cake with lemon and white
    chocolate 239–40
lentils: lentil stew with burnt aubergine,
    eggs, tahini and zehug 90–1
  Yemeni lentil meatballs 98
limes: coconut and lime pancakes with
    mango 52
  frozen meringue bar with strawberry
    and lime 184

M
maamool, Kalamata olive and orange 206
macadamias: medjool date, honey and
    macadamia breakfast loaf 156
mafrum, celeriac 152–53
maklooba, chicken 228–29
mangoes: amba relish 265
  amba sauce 266
  coconut and lime pancakes with
    mango 52
manouri cheese: roasted tomato and
    manouri cheese sandwich 143
mansaf, royal 234–35
marmalade and dried fruit cake 160
marunchinos 248
marzipan, pistachio, cardamom and
    rose 252
matbucha: chicken braised in spicy
    matbucha and cracked wheat pilaf
    103–4
meatballs: hedgehog meatballs 38
  spring lamb meatballs with broad
    beans and courgettes 95–6
  Yemeni lentil meatballs 98
meringues: frozen meringue bar with
    strawberry and lime 184
m'sabaha 145–46
mushroom scrambled eggs 27

N
nuts, roasting 276

O
olives: Kalamata olive and orange
    maamool 206

roasted Romano peppers, chickpeas,
    olives, roasted tomatoes and cumin
    210
onions: kamunia 200
oranges: chocolate pecan slice with
    oranges 245–46
  fennel, kohlrabi, orange and chilli
    salad 84
  Kalamata olive and orange maamool
    206
  white chocolate chip, currant and
    orange cookies 54

P
pancakes: coconut and lime pancakes
    with mango 52
parfait: frozen tahini parfait and
    chocolate sandwich cake 181–82
pasta: Israeli couscous with tomatoes,
    feta and lemon 36–7
pastilla, fish 225–26
pastry, walnut 76
peaches: baked custard fruit tart 186
  pickled peach salad with pistachios
    and parsley 169–70
peanut and cocoa nib brittle 250
pears: pear and saffron salad with
    walnut tahini 78–9
  pear and walnut upside-down cake
    163–64
peas: prawn, pea and potato tagine 50
pecans: chocolate pecan slice with
    oranges 245–46
peppers: pepper and chilli butter 108–9
  red pepper pickle 270
  red pepper, vine leaf and goat's cheese
    dolma cake 217–18
  roasted Romano peppers, chickpeas,
    olives, roasted tomatoes and cumin
    210
  tuna, capers and roasted pepper
    sandwich 143
phylas, spiced butternut squash 209
pickles: courgette pickle 267
  kohlrabi pickle 268
  pickled peach salad with pistachios
    and parsley 169–70
  quince pickle 268
  red cabbage pickle 270
  red pepper pickle 270
pide, fig and feta 128–29
pie, spinach, egg and filo 93
pilaf: cracked wheat 103–4
  royal mansaf 234–35

pilpelchuma 274
pistachios: cherry pistachio Bakewell 242
  pickled peach salad with pistachios
    and parsley 169–70
  pistachio and cranberry cake 161
  pistachio, cardamom and rose
    marzipan 252
  roasted carrots with pistachio cream,
    coriander seeds and honey 82
pitta bread: arayes 45
  crispy pitta shards 172
  sardines with roasted tomatoes and
    crispy pitta 177–78
plums: chicken in plums and sweet spice
    33–4
pomegranates: BBQ aubergine with
    jewelled rice salad 221–22
  cold yogurt and pomegranate soup
    174–75
posset, lemon and saffron 114
potatoes: potato and feta fritters 19
  prawn, pea and potato tagine 50
  tuna dip with broccoli, potato and
    eggs 70
prawn, pea and potato tagine 50
pumpkin: feather blade braised with
    pumpkin, spices and prunes 111–12
  pumpkin chirshi 201
  roasted spiced pumpkin with pickled
    apples 214–15

Q
quails with cannellini bean hummus,
    pepper and chilli butter 108–9
quince pickle 268

R
rabbit stifado 168
ras el hanout spice mix 263
red currants: chocolate cloud cake with
    red and black currants 117
red kidney beans: harira soup 20–1
relishes: amba relish 266
  fig relish 76
  zehug coriander relish 274
rice: BBQ aubergine with jewelled rice
    salad 221–22
  chicken maklooba 228–29
  hedgehog meatballs 38
  royal mansaf 234–35
  saffron carrot soup with a little bit of
    rice 26
ricotta: lemony ricotta dip 73–4
  strawberry ricotta cakes 118

rocket: lamb chops with rocket, figs and walnuts 232
Romanian white aubergine dip 69
rose water: pistachio, cardamom and rose marzipan 252
royal mansaf 234–35
runner beans: lamb tagine with runner beans and tomatoes 48

S
saffron: lemon and saffron posset 114
    pear and saffron salad with walnut tahini 78–9
    royal mansaf 234–35
    saffron carrot soup 26
salads: BBQ aubergine with jewelled rice salad 221–22
    brown wheat and broccoli salad with sesame dressing 89
    cherry, herb and freekeh tabule 212
    fennel, kohlrabi, orange and chilli salad 84
    pear and saffron salad with walnut tahini 78–9
    pickled peach salad with pistachios and parsley 169–70
    roasted spiced pumpkin with pickled apples 214–15
    steak fatoush salad with grapes and tomatoes 31
sandwiches: harissa and lemon chicken sandwich 142
    roasted tomato and manouri cheese sandwich 143
    tuna, capers and roasted pepper sandwich 143
    sardines with roasted tomatoes and crispy pitta 177–78
sauce, amba 266
sesame seeds: Jerusalem sesame bread 137–39
    sesame dressing 89
shakshuka, green 23–4
shata 273
shishbarak 149–50
shortbread, sumac and vanilla 56
side dishes 81–9
silky green aubergine purée 69
smoked haddock doughnuts 195–96
soups: cold tomato and basil soup 172
    cold yogurt and pomegranate soup 174–75
    harira soup 20–1
    saffron carrot soup 26

spices: amba spice mix 265
    Baharat spice mix 261
    chicken in plums and sweet spice 33–4
    honey and spice cookies 154
    ras el hanout spice mix 263
    sweet spice mix 260
spinach: green shakshuka 23–4
    spinach, egg and filo pie 93
stews: lamb stew with medjool dates 40
    lentil stew with burnt aubergine, eggs, tahini and zehug 90–1
    m'sabaha 145–46
    rabbit stifado 168
strawberries: frozen meringue bar with strawberry and lime 184
    strawberry ricotta cakes 118
sumac and vanilla shortbread 56
sweet spice mix 260
sweet zehug 275

T
tabule, cherry, herb and freekeh 212
tagines 46–51
    Essaouira fish tagine 49
    lamb tagine with runner beans and tomatoes 48
    prawn, pea and potato tagine 50
tahini: BBQ aubergine with jewelled rice salad 221–22
    fried cauliflower, amba and tahini sauce 86
    frozen tahini parfait and chocolate sandwich cake 181–82
    green tahini 272
    lamb stew with medjool dates (and sometimes tahini) 40
    lentil stew with burnt aubergine, eggs, tahini and zehug 90–1
    tahini cake with lemon and white chocolate 239–40
    walnut tahini 78–9
taramosalata 198
tarts: baked custard fruit tart 186
    cherry pistachio Bakewell 242
techniques 276–77
tomatoes: chicken braised in spicy matbucha and cracked wheat pilaf 103–4
    cold tomato and basil soup with crispy pitta shards 172
    Israeli couscous with tomatoes, feta and lemon 36–7
    lamb tagine with runner beans and tomatoes 48

roasted Romano peppers, chickpeas, olives, roasted tomatoes and cumin 210
    roasted tomato and manouri cheese sandwich 143
    sardines with roasted tomatoes and crispy pitta 177–78
    steak fatoush salad with grapes and tomatoes 31
    stuffed aubergine boats 100
tuna: tinned tuna cakes 42
    tuna, capers and roasted pepper sandwich 143
    tuna dip with broccoli, potato and eggs 70
Turkish yogurt bread with aubergine filling 133–34

V
vanilla: sumac and vanilla shortbread 56
vine leaves: red pepper, vine leaf and goat's cheese dolma cake 217–18

W
walnuts: lamb chops with rocket, figs and walnuts 232
    pear and walnut upside-down cake 163–64
    walnut pastry 76
    walnut tahini 78–9
wheat: brown wheat and broccoli salad 89

Y
Yemeni lentil meatballs 98
yogurt: cold yogurt and pomegranate soup 174–75
    royal mansaf 234–35
    shishbarak 149–50
    Turkish yogurt bread with aubergine filling 133–34

Z
zaalouk 67
zehug: lentil stew with burnt aubergine, eggs, tahini and zehug 90–1
    sweet zehug 275
    zehug coriander relish 274

Thank you

Our lives now are rich and hugely satisfying: we cook the food that we love for a living, we work with people whom we love dearly, we dance every day in our living room and we laugh all the time. But in life there are always questions that can't be answered, unsolvable problems, anxiety and stress, bad surprises. There is no manual, nor any guarantee; it's the people around us who help us power through. We are grateful to you all, but cannot name everyone here, so we will stick to just a few honorary mentions.

In Honey & Co: to Rachael Gibbon, our first employee ever, whom we love and adore, and to her front-of-house team; in the kitchen, to Julia Chodubska, an inspiration and a style goddess who made us believe we could leave the kitchen and it wouldn't collapse; and to Mirko d'Angelo, for reminding us that investing in people is our way forward and for the best hugs in the industry: stop stealing our moves.

In Honey & Spice: to Bridget Fojcik, our first true new friend in this country and a stellar shop manager; to Inbal Yeffet, an old friend who luckily decided to join us and help sort our life out; and of course, to Louisa Cornford, from her tiny office under the stairs to a fully grown-up office – she gives us her all every day, always there for us.

In Honey & Smoke: to Giorgia di Marzo, our first pastry chef and adopted daughter; to Paz and Gena, who run the kitchen; to Anthony who keeps the machine clean and moving, and still finds time for a little dance every day; and, on the floor, to Claudio, Camille, Jimmy and Sirio, who have a smile for everyone, and an extra one for us.

Then of course we want to thank everyone involved in this book, from Luigi Bonomi, who helped us find a new publisher, to everyone at said publisher, Pavilion, for your hard work and dedication to making this book: to Polly Powell and Katie Cowan for buying it, to Stephanie Milner for editing and to Laura Russell and Helen Lewis for getting it to look as good as possible. Daniel Fletcher and Charlie Phillips for interpreting our taste so well, plus a great thanks to Alex Gray, who helped us on the shoot. A huge one to Bryony Nowell for the meticulous attention, for making work fun and for the killer Palomas.

To Patricia Niven, whose beautiful pictures make our food look so good. We cannot articulate our love and gratitude to you, cannot imagine life without you.

To Shahar Argov, for fitting us in from time to time; you are the joy of our weeks.

To Natalie Whittle, Al Gilmour and all the incredible people at the *FT Weekend* for choosing us for their pages, where this book originated. We swell with pride every Saturday.

To Elizabeth Hallett and Alice Laurent, who have taught us so much about making books, and whose lessons will stay with us always.

From Itamar: to my brother Itay and mom Eilat, and to the incredible people who were with them in this difficult year: David Moses, Havi, Shosh, Shuli & Avi and Yoav & Esty Halevi, and to Dr. Benny Zuckerman. To Erez and Yonit, who have been there for me throughout. To my wife, Sarit, the source of all my happiness, my night and my day. There is no one in the world like you.

From Sarit: to my parents Hazel and Jeff, and my siblings and their partners, Tammy & Ofer and Shai & Edna, and to their amazing and fun kids: Eitan, Ayala, Avigail, Or, Lia and Osnat, for always being happy to eat and cook with me, and for being my cheerleaders. To my amazing loving husband, Itamar, for bringing our life into words that make me laugh and cry.

All our love to everyone that came to eat with us, everyone who cooked from our books and columns, everyone who wrote to us in response to something we have said or done – for better or worse – we are grateful for and humbled by the attention and hope to be worthy of it.